GOD'S DESIGN FOR

OUR PLANET EARTH

1:1

answersingenesis

Petersburg, Kentucky, USA

3RD EDITION | UPDATED, EXPANDED & FULL COLOR

ANSWERS IN GENESIS **SCIENCE** BY DEBBIE & RICHARD LAWRENCE

God's Design® for Heaven & Earth is a complete earth science curriculum for grades 1–8. The books in this series are designed for use in the Christian homeschool and Christian school, and provide easy-to-use lessons that will encourage children to see God's hand in everything around them.

Third edition
Second printing January 2010

Copyright © 2008 by Debbie and Richard Lawrence

ISBN: 1-60092-154-X

Cover design: Brandie Lucas & Diane King
Interior layout: Diane King
Editors: Lori Jaworski, Gary Vaterlaus

Published by Answers in Genesis, 2800 Bullittsburg Church Rd., Petersburg KY 41080

Printed in China

You may contact the authors at: info@rdeducation.com or (970) 686-5744

www.answersingenesis.org • www.godsdesignscience.com

PHOTO CREDITS

TABLE OF CONTENTS

Welcome to
God's Design® for Heaven & Earth

You are about to start an exciting series of lessons on earth science. *God's Design® for Heaven and Earth* consists of three books: *Our Universe*, *Our Planet Earth*, and *Our Weather and Water*. Each of these books will give you insight into how God designed and created our world and the universe in which we live.

No matter what grade you are in, first through eighth grade, you can use this book.

1st–2nd grade

Read only the "Beginner" section of each lesson, answer the questions at the end of that section, and then do the activity in the ⬤ box (the worksheets will be provided by your teacher).

3rd–5th grade

Skip the "Beginner" section and read the regular part of the lesson. After you read the lesson, do the activity in the ⬤ box and test your understanding by answering the questions in the ▬ box.

6th–8th grade

Skip the "Beginner" section and read the regular part of the lesson. After you read the lesson, do the activity in the ⬤ box and test your understanding by answering the questions in the ▬ box. Also do the "Challenge" section in the ⬤ box. This part of the lesson will challenge you to go beyond just elementary knowledge and do more advanced activities and learn additional interesting information.

Everyone should read the Special Features and do the final project. There are also unit quizzes and a final test to take.

Throughout this book you will see special icons like the one to the right. These icons tell you how the information in the lessons fit into the Seven C's of History: Creation, Corruption, Catastrophe, Confusion, Christ, Cross, Consummation. Your teacher will explain these to you.

Let's get started learning about God's design of our amazing earth!

UNIT 1

ORIGINS & GLACIERS

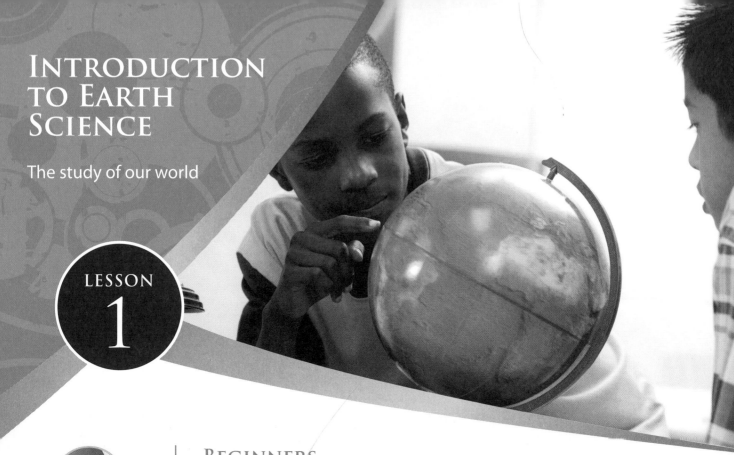

INTRODUCTION TO EARTH SCIENCE

The study of our world

LESSON 1

What does earth science include and why should we study it?

Words to know:

astronomy

meteorology

geology

lithosphere

hydrology

first law of thermodynamics

second law of thermodynamics

Challenge words:

evolution

BEGINNERS

We all live on a planet called *earth*, and you are about to begin a study of earth science, which is learning about the planet earth. There are many questions we can ask about the earth. Where do rocks come from? How is a cave formed? What makes a volcano erupt? We will learn the answers to these questions and many other things as we study about the earth.

The most important thing you can know about the earth is that God created it. In the Bible, in Genesis 1:1 it says, "In the beginning God created the heavens and the earth." The Bible tells us that God created the sun, moon, stars, sky, dry land, and every kind of plant and animal. So as you learn about the earth, look for things that God made. You will find that He created a really wonderful place for us to live.

- **What is earth science?**
- **Where did the earth come from?**
- **What other things did God create?**

W e all know where the earth is—it's all around us, right? We all know what it is—it's the planet we live on. Yet even though we are familiar with the planet we call earth and we see it every day, there are many questions that you may have about the earth. Where do rocks come from? How is a cave formed? What makes a volcano erupt? Why does it rain? How far away are the stars? Where did the universe come from? Earth science is the study of our world, and through this study scientists have attempted to answer many questions that people ask about the earth. Science has been able to answer some of these questions better than others.

Scientists break the study of the earth into four general categories. First, there is **astronomy**, the study of the space in which the earth exists. Second, there is **meteorology**, the study of the atmosphere surrounding the planet. Then there is **geology**, the study of the **lithosphere**, or the actual solid earth itself. Finally, there is **hydrology**, the study of the water on the earth. All of these studies help us to understand the wonderful world God has created for us to live on.

Although studying each of these areas will help you understand and appreciate the world on which you live, science can never answer all of your questions about the earth. We have to trust God's Word to answer some of our questions. For

THE EARTH IS RELIABLE

God created the earth with reliable laws in place. As we study earth science, we can see these laws at work. Of the many physical laws at work on earth, there are two that are particularly important to understand God's plan for the earth. The first, called the first law of thermodynamics, says that matter cannot be created or destroyed, only changed in form. This means that the things we see on the earth had to have come from something already existing. Only God can create something from nothing.

Another important physical law, the second law of thermodynamics, states that all objects tend to go to a state of rest or disorganization, called entropy. That means that the universe is gradually slowing down and everything is losing energy.

Purpose: To demonstrate the principle of increasing entropy

Materials: tennis ball, string, tape

Procedure:

1. Take a tennis ball and hold it in one hand. Hold your arm straight out in front of you and release the ball onto a hard surface. What does the ball do?

2. Now make a pendulum by taking a string and tying one end around the ball.

3. Use masking tape to tape the other end of the string to the top of a doorway so that the ball hangs at about the same height as your chin.

4. Take one step back from the doorway and gently pull the ball up until it just touches the tip of your nose. Then release it without pushing it. Be sure to stand very still. Did the ball hit you on the nose?

Conclusion:

After you dropped the ball, it bounced a few times and eventually came to rest on the floor as it lost its kinetic energy. The ball on the pendulum swung out and back without actually touching you. This is because the ball is losing energy as it swings through the air; eventually it will stop.

We observe these same principles at work on a large scale when we study planets and galaxies, and on a tiny scale when we study molecules and atoms. The Bible says that God created the universe and upholds it by His power (Hebrews 1:3; Colossians 1:17). He designed our world in an orderly way, and we can trust Him to take care of it and us.

instance, science cannot prove where the earth came from. There are many ideas or theories that we will examine, but none of them scientifically proves where the earth came from. Only the Bible can answer that question. Genesis 1:1–2 says "In the beginning God created the heavens and the earth. The earth was without form, and void; and darkness was on the face of the deep. And the Spirit of God was hovering over the face of the waters." The Bible tells us that God created the sun, moon, stars, sky, dry land, and every kind of plant and animal. Since no man was there and scientists cannot recreate the beginning of the world, we must trust God's Word to tell us what happened.

As you study earth science, you will find God's mighty hand all around you. Romans 1:19–20 says, "what may be known of God is manifest in them [men], for God has shown it to them. For since the creation of the world His invisible attributes are clearly seen, being understood by the things that are made, even His eternal power and Godhead, so that they are without excuse." So look for evidence of God in the world around you. You won't be disappointed. ■

WHAT DID WE LEARN?

- What are the four main studies of earth science?
- What is one question mentioned in this lesson that science cannot answer about the earth?
- Why can we rely on God's Word to tell us where the earth came from?

TAKING IT FURTHER

- How does the first law of thermodynamics confirm the Genesis account of creation?
- How does the second law of thermodynamics confirm the Genesis account of creation?
- Read Psalm 139:8–10. What do these verses say about where we can find God?

IS EVOLUTION SCIENTIFIC?

As you begin to study earth science, you will find that most of the books, magazines, and videos that you get from the public library or from a public school classroom state that the earth and the universe are billions of years old, that life evolved from nonlife, and that there is no power at work in nature except the natural things that we see and can test. These ideas are all part of a worldview called **evolution**. But these evolutionary ideas do not fit with the Word of God. The Bible clearly says that God created the earth, the universe, and all forms of life. It says that God created everything from nothing and that He did it in six days, and then rested on the seventh day. And the Bible indicates that this all took place only a few thousand years ago.

So what are we to believe? First, let's read some quotes from some evolutionists and look at what they have to say about the situation. After reading each quote below, write a summary of what that person is saying about his belief in evolution.

Professor Richard Lewontin is a geneticist and one of the world's leaders in evolutionary biology.

"We take the side of science *in spite of* the patent absurdity of some of its constructs, *in spite of* its failure to fulfill many of its extravagant promises of health and life, *in spite of* the tolerance of the scientific community for unsubstantiated just-so stories, because we have a prior commitment, a commitment to materialism. It is not that the methods and institutions of science somehow compel us to accept a material explanation of the phenomenal world, but, on the contrary, that we are forced by our *a priori* adherence to material causes to create an apparatus of investigation and a set of concepts that produce material explanations, no matter how counter-intuitive, no matter how mystifying to the uninitiated. Moreover, that materialism is an absolute, for we cannot allow a Divine Foot in the door."[1]

Aldous Huxley was a British novelist who wrote *Brave New World* (1932). He came from a family of evolutionists. Below is a quote explaining his view of life.

"I had motive for not wanting the world to have a meaning; consequently assumed that it had none, and was able without any difficulty to find satisfying reasons for this assumption. The philosopher who finds no meaning in the world is not concerned exclusively with a problem in pure metaphysics, he is also concerned to prove that there is no valid reason why he personally should not do as he wants to do, or why his friends should not seize political power and govern

in the way that they find most advantageous to themselves. . . . For myself, the philosophy of meaninglessness was essentially an instrument of liberation, sexual and political."[2]

Geoffrey Burbidge is a renowned astrophysicist and had the following to say about the big bang theory.

"Big bang cosmology is probably as widely believed as has been any theory of the universe in the history of Western civilization. It rests, however, on many untested, and in some cases untestable, assumptions. Indeed, big bang cosmology has become a bandwagon of thought that reflects faith as much as objective truth."[3]

This final quote is from Michael Ruse who was a professor of philosophy and zoology at the University of Geulph in Canada. What is he saying about evolution?

"Evolution is promoted by its practitioners as more than mere science. Evolution is promulgated as an ideology, a secular religion—a full-fledged alternative to Christianity, with meaning and morality. I am an ardent evolutionist and an ex-Christian, but I must admit that in this one complaint—and Mr [*sic*] Gish is but one of many to make it—the literalists are absolutely right. Evolution is a religion. This was true of evolution in the beginning, and it is true of evolution still today.

". . . Evolution therefore came into being as a kind of secular ideology, an explicit substitute for Christianity."[4]

Are you surprised by what these men had to say? Richard Lewontin is saying that scientists must believe in materialism to keep the Divine Foot, or God, from entering the picture. He says that there are many unsubstantiated stories and that the evidence does not necessarily compel scientists to believe in evolution.

Huxley is saying that he assumed the world has no meaning, so that he could develop a world where he could do whatever he wanted. This is the result of evolutionary thinking. If there is no God, then there is no reason not to do whatever you want. You will see a strict adherence to evolution in many people's writings because it provides a world with no meaning and thus no moral restrictions.

What Dr. Burbidge is saying is that the belief in the big bang is exactly that, a belief. There are many assumptions being used to "prove" the big bang that cannot be tested, and really don't prove anything.

Finally, Dr. Ruse is openly admitting that evolution is a religion that can be substituted for Christianity. Keep these ideas in mind when you read books that promote evolution as true. Often the things evolutionists claim to be facts are really only assumptions that are required to support the religion of evolution.

1   Richard Lewontin, "Billions and Billions of Demons," *The New York Review*, January 9, 1997, p. 31.

2   Aldous Huxley, *Ends and Means* (New York: Harper, 1937), pp. 270 ff.
3   Geoffrey Burbidge, "Why Only One Big Bang?" *Scientific American* 266 no. 2 (1992): 96.

4   Michael Ruse, "How Evolution Became a Religion," *National Post*, May 13, 2000.

INTRODUCTION TO GEOLOGY

The study of the earth itself

LESSON 2

What is geology and how does it affect us?

Words to know:

physical geology

geophysics

mineralogy

sedimentology

paleontology

environmental geology

BEGINNERS

Geology sounds like a big word, but what it really means is the study of the earth. In this book you are going to learn some things about the earth. What do you know about the earth? It has soil and rocks. It also has mountains and volcanoes. You will get to learn about all those things as you go through the lessons in this book. You will also learn about earthquakes and glaciers.

All of these things help make earth a special place. God made the earth with a lot of liquid water, which is something that no other planet has. He also placed the earth just the right distance from the sun to keep the temperature from getting too hot or too cold. Aren't you glad that God made the earth the way He did?

Almost everything you use, eat, or buy comes from the earth in one way or another. The food you eat was grown in the soil on the earth. The cars you ride in are made from metal that is mined from the earth. Plastic that is used in your toothbrush or drinking cup comes from oil that is pumped from below the surface of the earth. Did you know that the earth was so important? If you look around and think about where things come from, you find that everything comes from the planet that God made for us.

- What is geology?

- What makes earth a special planet?

- What are some things around you that came from the earth?

Geology is the study of the planet earth. It is the study of the structures that form the earth, the processes affecting those structures, as well as the physical history of the planet. For example, geologists study soil, rocks, mountains, and volcanoes. They try to locate particular minerals. They study and try to predict earthquakes. Geologists study glaciers and how they move. And geologists study the interaction between water, atmosphere, and the earth's surface.

The earth was perfectly designed by God to support life. What are some of the things that make earth unique? First, it contains just the right elements. No other place in our solar system has abundant liquid water, which is crucial for supporting life. Water is one of the few substance that is less dense after it freezes, allowing ice to form on the surface of lakes instead of from the bottom up, so fish and other aquatic life can survive the freezing cold. Water is a nearly universal dissolver, allowing most chemical reactions to occur. The earth is also the only planet with just the right amount of oxygen in the atmosphere to support life—too little and we would suffocate, too much and fires would burn out of control.

The earth has just the right mass to give us the needed gravity. Gravity holds the atmosphere around our planet so that we can breathe and have protection from the extreme temperatures of space. Gravity provides the needed air pressure for our bodies to function properly.

The earth is just the right distance from the sun and has just the right rotation to support life. If the earth were closer to the sun, all the water would boil away. If it were farther away, the water would all freeze. The tilt of the earth and its revolution around the sun allow for the seasons, which provide the needed growing time for all the food we consume. All of these special features did not just happen by chance. They were the result of a loving God, who wanted to create a wonderful world for us.

You may not think geology is important to you, but geology affects your life in many ways every day. The nutrients and minerals in your food are a result of geology. Metals are used to make many things you use every day, such as tools, cars, and buildings. Petroleum is used to make gasoline to power your car, and it is used to make the many plastic items around your house. Sand is used to make glass, not to mention sand castles. And glaciers carved many of the mountain passes that we see. So you can't avoid geology.

FUN FACT

Many of the sayings we hear have a geology basis. For example: "solid as a rock"; "I was petrified"; "That really rocks" and "Sink like a rock." Can you think of other common sayings that are related to the earth? (Crystal clear, pure gold, far above rubies, etc.)

GEOLOGY SCAVENGER HUNT

Using a copy of "Geology Scavenger Hunt" worksheet, identify each item that is commonly found around most homes.

If geology really interests you, consider one of the following fields of geology:

- **Physical Geology**—study of rocks, magma, the earth's core, land formations

- **Geophysics**—study of the earth's magnetic fields, heat flow, gravity, seismic waves

- **Mineralogy**—study of minerals in the earth's crust, moon rocks, crystals

- **Sedimentology/Paleontology**—study of sediment deposits, fossils

- **Environmental Geology**—study of the effects of humans on the earth's environment ■

WHAT DID WE LEARN?

- What is geology?
- What are some of the evidences that God designed the earth uniquely to support life?

TAKING IT FURTHER

- List some ways that geology affects your life on a regular basis.
- What area of geology interests you the most?

ELEMENTS

Everything on earth is made from basic building blocks called elements. You can learn about the elements by studying a periodic table of the elements. Some of the elements you already learned about in the scavenger hunt. Other elements are less well known. You have certainly learned about silver and gold, but you may not be familiar with tantalum, osmium, or polonium. The first 92 elements listed on the periodic table are naturally occurring on the earth. The rest are man-made elements. Look at the periodic table of the elements on the next page and study it. See which elements you are familiar with and which ones you have never heard of. See which ones are naturally occurring and which ones have been made by man.

As we mentioned earlier, the food you eat contains minerals or elements that are found in the crust of the earth. Look at labels on the food in your kitchen and see how many elements you can find.

PERIODIC TABLE OF THE ELEMENTS

Legend (cell key):
- Atomic number 12
- Symbol .... MG
- Atomic Mass 24.31
- Name .... Magnesium
- Electron structure by energy level 2,8,2

Categories:
- Alkali metals
- Alkali-earth metals
- Transition metals
- Poor metals
- Metalloids
- Nonmetals
- Noble gases
- Hydrogen nonmetal

Note: the lowest electron levels are not shown for rows 6 and 7, instead they are indicated by a -. In row 6 - means 2, 8, and in row 7 - means 2, 8, 18

Period	IA	IIA	IIIB	IVB	VB	VIB	VIIB	VIIIB	VIIIB	VIIIB	IB	IIB	IIIA	IVA	VA	VIA	VIIA	VIIIA
1	1 H 1.008 Hydrogen 1																	2 He 4.0026 Helium 2
2	3 Li 6.941 Lithium 2,1	4 Be 9.012 Beryllium 2,2											5 B 10.81 Boron 2,3	6 C 12.01 Carbon 2,4	7 N 14.01 Nitrogen 2,5	8 O 16 Oxygen 2,6	9 F 19 Fluorine 2,7	10 Ne 20.18 Neon 2,8
3	11 Na 22.99 Sodium 2,8,1	12 Mg 24.31 Magnesium 2,8,2											13 Al 26.98 Aluminum 2,8,3	14 Si 28.09 Silicon 2,8,4	15 P 30.97 Phosphorus 2,8,5	16 S 32.07 Sulfur 2,8,6	17 Cl 35.45 Chlorine 2,8,7	18 Ar 39.95 Argon 2,8,8
4	19 K 39.1 Potassium 2,8,8,1	20 Ca 40.08 Calcium 2,8,8,2	21 Sc 44.96 Scandium 2,8,9,2	22 Ti 47.9 Titanium 2,8,10,2	23 V 50.94 Vanadium 2,8,11,2	24 Cr 52 Chromium 2,8,13,1	25 Mn 54.94 Manganese 2,8,13,2	26 Fe 55.85 Iron 2,8,14,2	27 Co 58.93 Cobalt 2,8,15,2	28 Ni 58.69 Nickel 2,8,16,2	29 Cu 63.55 Copper 2,8,18,1	30 Zn 65.39 Zinc 2,8,18,2	31 Ga 69.72 Gallium 2,8,18,3	32 Ge 72.59 Germanium 2,8,18,4	33 As 74.92 Arsenic 2,8,18,5	34 Se 78.96 Selenium 2,8,18,6	35 Br 79.9 Bromine 2,8,18,7	36 Kr 83.8 Krypton 2,8,18,8
5	37 Rb 85.47 Rubidium 2,8,18,8,1	38 Sr 87.62 Strontium 2,8,18,8,2	39 Y 88.91 Yttrium 2,8,18,9,2	40 Zr 91.22 Zirconium 2,8,18,10,2	41 Nb 92.91 Niobium 2,8,18,12,1	42 Mo 95.94 Molybdenum 2,8,18,13,1	43 Tc 99 Technetium 2,8,18,14,1	44 Ru 101.1 Ruthenium 2,8,18,15,1	45 Rh 102.9 Rhodium 2,8,18,16,1	46 Pd 106.4 Palladium 2,8,18,17,1	47 Ag 107.9 Silver 2,8,18,1	48 Cd 112.4 Cadmium 2,8,18,2	49 In 114.8 Indium 2,8,18,3	50 Sn 118.7 Tin 2,8,18,4	51 Sb 121.8 Antimony 2,8,18,5	52 Te 127.6 Tellurium 2,8,18,6	53 I 126.9 Iodine 2,8,18,7	54 Xe 131.3 Xenon 2,8,18,8
6	55 Cs 132.9 Cesium -18,18,8,1	56 Ba 137.3 Barium -18,18,8,2	57 La 138.9 Lanthanum -18,18,9,2	72 Hf 178.5 Hafnium -18,32,10,2	73 Ta 180.9 Tantalum -18,32,11,2	74 W 183.9 Tungsten -18,32,12,2	75 Re 186.2 Rhenium -18,32,13,2	76 Os 190.2 Osmium -18,32,14,2	77 Ir 192.2 Iridium -18,32,15,2	78 Pt 195.1 Platinum -18,32,17,1	79 Au 197 Gold -18,32,18,1	80 Hg 200.5 Mercury -18,32,18,2	81 Tl 204.4 Thallium -18,32,18,3	82 Pb 207.2 Lead -18,32,18,4	83 Bi 209 Bismuth -18,32,18,5	84 Po (209) Polonium -18,32,18,6	85 At (210) Astatine -18,32,18,7	86 Rn (222) Radon -18,32,18,8
7	87 Fr (223) Francium -18,32,18,1	88 Ra (226) Radium -18,32,18,2	89 Ac (227) Actinium -18,32,18,9,2	104 Rf (261) Rutherfordium -18,32,10,2	105 Db (262) Dubnium -18,32,11,2	106 Sg 262.94 Seaborgium -18,32,12,2	107 Bh (264) Bohrium -18,32,13,2	108 Hs (265) Hassium -18,32,14,2	109 Mt (266) Meitnerium -18,32,15,2	110 Ds (271) Darmstadtium -18,32,17,1	111 Rg (280) Roentgenium -18,32,18,1	112 Uub (285) Ununbium -18,32,18,2	113 Uut (284) Ununtrium -18,32,18,3	114 Uuq (289) Ununquadium -18,32,18,4	115 Uup (288) Ununpentium -18,32,18,5	116 Uuh (?) Ununhexium -18,32,18,6	117 Uus (?) Ununseptium -18,32,18,7	118 Uuo (?) Ununoctium -18,32,18,8

Lanthanides (row 6):

58 Ce 140.1 Cerium -18,20,8,2	59 Pr 140.9 Praseodymium -18,21,8,2	60 Nd 144.2 Neodymium -18,22,8,2	61 Pm (145) Promethium -18,23,8,2	62 Sm 150.4 Samarium -18,24,8,2	63 Eu 152 Europium -18,25,8,2	64 Gd 157.3 Gadolinium -18,25,9,2	65 Tb 158.9 Terbium -18,27,8,2	66 Dy 162.5 Dysprosium -18,28,8,2	67 Ho 164.9 Holmium -18,29,8,2	68 Er 167.3 Erbium -18,30,8,2	69 Tm 168.9 Thulium -18,31,8,2	70 Yb 173 Ytterbium -18,32,8,2	71 Lu 175 Lutetium -18,32,9,2

Actinides (row 7):

90 Th 232 Thorium -18,32,18,10,2	91 Pa 233 Protactinium -18,32,20,9,2	92 U 238 Uranium -18,32,21,9,2	93 Np (237) Neptunium -18,32,22,9,2	94 Pu (244) Plutonium -18,32,24,8,2	95 Am (243) Americium -18,32,25,8,2	96 Cm (247) Curium -18,32,25,9,2	97 Bk (247) Berkelium -18,32,26,9,2	98 Cf (251) Californium -18,32,28,8,2	99 Es (252) Einsteinium -18,32,29,8,2	100 Fm (257) Fermium -18,32,30,8,2	101 Md (258) Mendelevium -18,32,31,8,2	102 No (259) Nobelium -18,32,32,8,2	103 Lr (262) Lawrencium -18,32,32,9,2

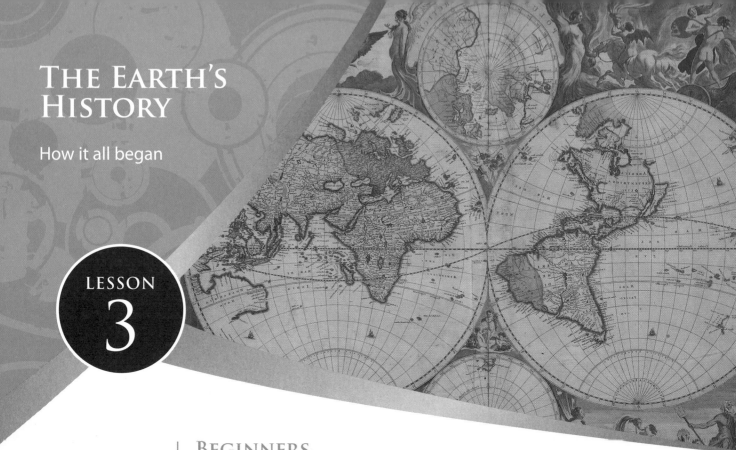

THE EARTH'S HISTORY

How it all began

How was the earth shaped throughout its history?

Words to know:

uniformitarianism

polystrate fossil

Challenge words:

theistic evolution

BEGINNERS

The earth as we see it today came about because of three very important events. First, God created the earth. You can read about this in the first chapter of your Bible. It says that God created the heavens and the earth and that they were very good. The second important event that affected the earth was when Adam and Eve disobeyed God (Genesis 3). As part of their punishment, God cursed the earth. The earth is different from the way God originally created it. One way that it is different is that it now produces weeds and thorns, making it difficult to grow the plants that we want.

The third important event that changed the way the earth looks is the Genesis Flood that happened when Noah was alive (Genesis 6–8). Water covered the whole earth and changed the way the earth looks. We will learn more about how the Flood affected the earth in the next lesson.

From the Bible we learn that the earth is about 6,000 years old, but not everyone believes this. Many people believe the earth is very old, even billions of years old. They do not believe that there was a worldwide flood; instead, they believe it took a very long time for the earth to become the way it is. Since scientists disagree on how the earth came to be the way it is, we must choose to believe what the Bible says. When we look at fossils, rocks, and other evidence, it supports what the Bible says.

- What are the three important events that have shaped the earth?

- Does the Bible indicate that the earth is thousands or billions of years old?

No human was around to witness the beginning of the earth. And science has been unable to recreate the processes showing how the earth was formed. Therefore, people have developed many ideas about how it all began and how the earth ended up the way it is today. Among the many ideas that have been proposed, two are the most popular.

Belief systems

Creation scientists believe the biblical account of creation. The Bible says that the earth, as it is today, is the result of three important events.

1. Creation: Genesis 1 says that God created the heavens and the earth and that they were "very good."

2. The Fall: Adam and Eve sinned and God cursed the earth. The earth was changed from what it originally was (Genesis 3:17–19; Romans 8:20–22).

3. The Flood: God flooded the entire earth as judgment for man's wickedness (Genesis 6–8). Profound changes occurred to the earth, its atmosphere, and all of nature because of this Flood.

From the Bible, we learn that the earth is only about six thousand years old and that it was "very good" when it was created. The earth we see today has been deeply affected by the Fall of man and the Genesis Flood.

Evolutionary scientists have a naturalistic view—that nature is all there is and everything happened by natural processes. They deny that there is a God that created everything. They believe that the earth is billions of years old and that life is the result of slow, natural evolution—with one kind of animal changing into another. They believe in **uniformitarianism**. This is the belief that all changes to the earth have been brought about by the processes we see today. For example, evolutionists surmise that since we observe slow erosion today, that features such as mountains and valleys must have resulted from millions or even billions of years of slow erosion. They deny a worldwide, catastrophic flood.

Evidence

Neither creation nor evolution can be scientifically proven. We must trust what God has said in His Word—He is the only eyewitness to creation! However, when we do look at the clues the earth gives us, we see that they confirm what the Bible teaches. Let's look at a few examples.

- Fossils—billions of dead things, mostly aquatic (water plants and animals), found in rock layers in every part of the earth, including on tops of mountains, in deserts, and even in Antarctica

- Large deposits of coal and oil—remains of once-living plants and animals

- Evidence of an ice age, with many glaciers remaining

- Strata—many layers of different rock stacked on top of each other

How do we best account for these observations?

The Bible says there was a worldwide Flood. This would have rapidly eroded the surface of the earth, depositing layers of sediment over every part of the earth and burying billions of organisms. This rapid covering would account for the many layers of sedimentary rock over the earth as well as the vast number of fossils in them discovered around the world. It would also account for the large oil and coal deposits that have been discovered. Finally, conditions after the Flood would have been just right to trigger an ice age.

The Flood also would have deposited large amounts of sediment in the ocean. If we figure the age of the oceans by the current rate of deposition, the sediment in the oceans would have been accumulating for less than 12 million years. This time period is much shorter than the 4.5 billion years that evolutionists claim for the age of the earth, and there is no plausible explanation for why there is not more sediment in the oceans if the earth is really billions of years old. This 12 million years is much longer than the Bible teaches that the earth has been around, but it is a maximum age, not the actual age. The Flood with its raging waters and worldwide scope would account for most of the sediment in the ocean.

Problems with evolution

Evolutionists explain that the layers of rock containing fossils formed slowly over millions of years. However, fossils only form when a creature is quickly covered with mud or sand shortly after it dies. Slow, gradual covering does not result in fossils because the dead animal is eaten by other animals or decays before it can become fossilized. Without a large-scale disaster, such as the Genesis Flood, fossils do not form very often. So evolutionists explain the abundance of fossils by saying they formed over very long periods of time. Also, the fossils of aquatic (water) creatures found on the tops of even the tallest mountains and in the deserts can be explained by the Genesis Flood. Evolutionists try to say that the level of the oceans has risen and fallen as the climate slowly changes, and that the mountains were slowly uplifted over millions of years. However, we do not observe these kinds of changes happening today.

Uniformitarianism also cannot explain how such vast amounts of coal and oil were formed when we do not see significant amounts being formed now. Just as with fossils, coal and oil are formed when plants are covered quickly and then compressed. This is more consistent with a catastrophe than with slow uniform processes.

Evolutionists say that there have been many ice ages in the past. Yet they cannot explain what triggers them or how they form. Cooler temperatures do not provide enough moisture for an ice age. So a slowly changing climate would not trigger an ice age with the formation of giant glaciers. However, the conditions necessary for the Ice Age would be just right after the Flood, due to lower temperatures on the continents and more moisture available from oceans that were warmer than today's oceans.

Finally, some areas of rock strata have layers that are not in the "right order" according to evolutionary time scales. And other strata have fossilized tree trunks that are upright through many layers of sediment that are thought to be separated

FLOOD IN A JAR

Purpose: To demonstrate how a flood sorts objects

Materials: large jar with lid, sand, dirt, pebbles, rocks, water

Procedure:

1. Put a handful of sand, a handful of dirt, a handful of pebbles, and a few larger rocks into a large jar. You can add some sticks, twigs, leaves, and grass as well. Do not fill the jar more than half full.

2. Fill the jar with water to within an inch of the top and tighten the lid.

3. Shake the jar for 30 seconds, and then set the jar on a level area. Observe what happens as the materials in the water settle to the bottom of the jar.

4. Wait 30 minutes and observe the jar again.

Questions:

- What did the jar look like right after you shook it?

- What do you see happening in the jar after 30 minutes?

- Did any of the leaves or twigs get buried in the mud and sand?

Conclusion:

You should observe the heavy items settling first, then the lighter items settling later. This forms layers of different materials in the bottom of the jar. This is like the layers we see in sedimentary rock formations today (shown here). The leaves and twigs that were buried illustrate how some of the plants and animals were buried during the Flood and became fossils.

by millions of years. Fossils that go through many layers of sediment are called **polystrate fossils**. Obviously, the trees could not have fossilized over millions of years; they would have decayed long before that, so they must have been buried rapidly and the sedimentary layers must have formed rapidly. Scientists who believe in uniformitarianism often contradict themselves and each other, and they ignore much of the data that does not support their ideas.

As a Christian, you must believe God's Word and look at the world through "biblical glasses." The Bible explains where the world came from, why it looks like it does now, and what will happen in the future. And as a good scientist, you should carefully examine all the data. When interpreted according to biblical history, all the data we have confirms what the Bible teaches. God's Word is ever true! ∎

This fossilized tree in Grand Canyon extends through multiple layers of sedimentary rock.

WHAT DID WE LEARN?

- What are the two most popular views for how the earth became what it is today?

- According to the Bible, what are the three major events that affected the way the earth looks today?

- Should a good scientist disregard evidence that contradicts his/her ideas?

- Have scientists proven that evolution is true?

- Have scientists proven that biblical creation is true?

TAKING IT FURTHER

- How might scientists explain the discovery of fossilized seashells in the middle of a desert?

- Explain how a fossilized tree could be found upright through several layers of rock.

- For more evidence for a young earth, go to www.answersingenesis.org/go/young.

IS GENESIS HISTORY?

In the lesson we said that there are two basic views on how the earth came to be the way it is today, but there really is a third view that is becoming more popular. This view is called **theistic evolution**. People who hold this view claim that they believe the Bible, and they believe that the earth is billions of years old and living things evolved from simpler organisms changed over these long ages. They do not see a conflict between these two statements. They say that they believe the Bible because they believe that the account of creation given in Genesis is just figurative; that the story is poetic in nature and not to be taken literally.

Now there are many passages in the Bible that are poetic in nature. There are songs, psalms, and proverbs that are not literal history. Some of

these poetic passages occur in the middle of books that are generally considered narrative or historical. So how can we tell if the account in Genesis chapters 1 and 2 is literal history or just poetic in nature?

When one examines the language used in Genesis 1–2, it has all the characteristics of historical narrative, not poetry or parable. This includes the Hebrew grammatical structure, the verbs used, the word order, etc. Plus, the New Testament writers, and Jesus Himself, refer to the events of creation, the Fall of Adam and Eve, and the Flood as real historical events.

Why is it important to believe that the world was created in six literal days? If you believe that the earth is billions of years old, even if you believe God created the earth and the things in it, you believe that

death occurred before Adam sinned, since there are millions of fossils on earth that would have been formed before Adam. But the Bible says that death was the punishment for man's sin. It is difficult to reconcile the belief in an old earth with the belief in death as a punishment for sin and thus man's need for a savior. If you choose to take the creation account in Genesis as a figurative example and not literal history, how do you know when to start taking the rest of the Bible's history literally? It is important to believe the history of the Bible so that we can believe in the Savior of the Bible. Science does not confirm that the earth is old as you will learn as you study geology. You can find out more about why Genesis should be taken as history at www.answersingenesis.org/go/literal.

DATING METHODS

How can we tell how old the earth is? Don't scientific dating methods prove that the earth is billions of years old? You might believe this if you read magazine articles, books, or the newspaper. Most dates for fossils, rocks, and other geological formations are stated as if they are proven facts. However, this is not the case. Let's examine how these dating methods work and we will see that science has not proven the earth to be more than a few thousand years old.

There are three main ways that scientists try to date different objects. Various radiometric dating methods, ones measuring elements with radioactive decay, are used for dating igneous and metamorphic rocks. Carbon-14 dating is a common method used for dating organic materials. And index fossils are used to date sedimentary rocks. All of these methods have significant problems that are often overlooked. Most of these problems lie in the assumptions that are made in order to use the dating method. Radiometric and carbon-14 dating rely on three assumptions:

1. The rate of decay of the element being measured is constant.

2. The system is isolated—none of the material being measured has entered or left the sample by any other means than radioactive decay.

3. The initial conditions are known—the scientist assumes he knows how much of the material being measured was in the sample at the time it was formed.

Let's look as how these assumptions work with each of these methods. One common type of radiometric dating is uranium-lead dating. This method uses the fact that uranium-238 is unstable and decays to become lead-206 at a fixed rate. Half of a sample of U-238 will become Pb-206 in 4.47 billion years (this is called its half-life). Scientists have measured this rate of decay over the past ninety years or so, so we'll assume that the rate of decay is constant.

As for the second assumption, rock samples do not exist in an isolated system. Elements can leach in and out of rock areas, especially if water is flowing through them. Many samples are rejected for testing if they are suspected of contamination. And if results are unexpected, the sample is usually classified as contaminated.

And finally, it is assumed that igneous rocks have known quantities of lead in them when they are made. Therefore, any extra lead in the sample is assumed to be there because of the decay of the uranium. However, many tests on lava flows with known eruption dates have proven this to be inaccurate. For example, Indians living in Arizona about 900 years ago recorded volcanic eruptions in the area and tree rings in the area indicate that the eruptions took place about 900 years ago. When rock samples from this area were tested using radioisotope methods, they were dated at 210,000–230,000 years old. There was a much higher lead content than would be expected for rocks that are less than a thousand years old. But this is not an isolated incident. Rocks from a lava flow in Hawaii that occurred between 1800 and 1801 were dated with various methods and were given 12 different dates ranging from 1.4 million years to 2.96 billion years. None of the radiometric dating methods was even close to the actual date of only 200 years. Thus we can see that radioisotope dating is not reliable.

Carbon-14 dating has similar problems. C-14 is made when cosmic rays knock neutrons out of atomic nuclei in the upper atmosphere. These displaced neutrons, now moving fast, hit ordinary nitrogen (N-14) at lower altitudes, converting it into C-14. When C-14 has been formed, it behaves just like ordinary carbon (carbon-12), combining with oxygen to give carbon dioxide, and also gets freely cycled through the cells of all plants and animals. Unlike common carbon, however, C-14 is unstable and slowly decays, changing back to nitrogen and releasing energy. This instability makes it radioactive. Only living things contain C-14, and when an organism dies, the amount of C-14 decays slowly over time. By measuring the amount of C-14 left, a date of death is determined. Three assumptions are made in this dating technique: 1) the ratio of carbon-14 to carbon-12 in living things has been constant; 2) any change in the amount of C-14 in a substance is due entirely to radioactive decay; and 3) the decay rate of C-14 has been constant. We know that the production of C-14 can be affected by solar radiation, the earth's magnetic field, and volcanic activity. And carbon can leach out of a substance. The Flood, also, would have greatly upset the carbon balance by burying much plant material containing carbon.

Examples abound of items of known date that have given obviously wrong results when using carbon dating. For example, a freshly killed seal was dated as having died 1,300 years ago, and a living mollusk shell was dated as being 2,300 years old. With many examples of incorrect results, other results must be suspect as well. Finally, the carbon in a sample is almost completely gone in about 60,000 years, so samples cannot be tested with C-14 to prove extremely old dates. This creates another problem for old-earth scientists. Many items such as diamonds and coal, which are supposed to be millions of years old, have been found to contain C-14. If they were truly millions of years old, any C-14 that was originally in the sample would have decayed.

Because sedimentary rocks are made from bits of other rocks, radiometric dating does not usually work on them. Therefore, sedimentary rocks are often dated by examining the fossils contained in them and then matching them to index fossils. An index fossil is always a particular fossil species that is found buried in rock layers over a very wide geographical area. Furthermore, the same fossil species must have a narrow vertical distribution, that is, only be buried in a few rock layers. The evolutionist interprets this as meaning that the species lived and died over a relatively short time (perhaps a few million years). Therefore, the rock layers containing these fossils supposedly only represent that relatively short period of time, and thus a "date" can be assigned according to the rock layers where these fossils are found. The "date" relative to other index fossils and rock layers is, of course, determined by the species' position in the evolutionary "tree of life" according to the order of fossils in rock layer sequences. Using the fossil in the rock sample to date the rock and then using the rock layer to date the index fossil is called circular reasoning and is bad logic.

There are other radiometric methods as well, including potassium-argon, rubidium-strontium, and thorium-lead, but all such methods used for dating rocks and organic samples have significant problems and results are often thrown out or labeled as contaminated or unreliable. Therefore, we must be careful when we read or hear that something has been determined to be millions or billions of years old. Old ages for the earth cannot be reliably confirmed. The Bible indicates that the earth is only about 6,000 years old.

THE GENESIS FLOOD

God's punishment for sin

LESSON 4

How did the Genesis Flood affect the earth?

BEGINNERS

When Noah was alive, a few thousand years ago, God became angry with the wickedness of the people. He determined to destroy all but eight people: Noah, his wife, their three sons, and their sons' wives. God told Noah to build an Ark, which was a very large boat. God sent two of each kind of animal (and seven of some) that lived on the land to the Ark. Once all the animals and Noah and his family were on the Ark, God shut the door. God sent a great Flood that covered the entire world, and all of the people and animals that lived on the land died.

The waters that flowed over the land carried mud and dirt with them. This dirt and mud covered over many of the animals that had been alive, and eventually these animals turned into fossils. Also much of the dirt and other debris that was left behind by the floodwaters turned into rocks. The water also washed away rock and dirt in many areas, changing the way the earth looks. Much of what we see when we study the earth today is a result of this great Flood.

After the Flood, the climate was different than before. It is believed that before the Flood, the earth was generally warm and tropical. But after the Flood, it was much cooler. There were a lot more clouds and there was probably a lot of ash in the air from erupting volcanoes. This change in climate could have caused the great Ice Age.

- Why did God send the Genesis Flood?

- How did the Flood affect the surface of the earth?

- How was the weather different after the Flood?

According to the Bible, how the earth looks today is not the same as how the earth looked at creation. Two major catastrophes have led to changes that have greatly affected the surface of the earth. The first change happened as a result of Adam's sin against God in the Garden of Eden. Genesis 3:17–19 says that God cursed the ground, causing it to grow thorns and thistles. The original plan for the earth was for it to produce food without weeds. But all this changed as a result of man's sin.

The second catastrophe was also a result of man's sin. Genesis 6:3–8 says that man had become so wicked that God determined to flood the entire earth to destroy the human race. Noah and his family were the only humans saved from the Flood.

This worldwide Flood not only killed all air-breathing, land-dwelling animals not on board the Ark, but made major changes to the face of the earth. Layers of sediment were quickly laid down all over the world, resulting in the sedimentary rock formations and multitudes of fossils that we see today.

It is probable that the Flood was associated with the breaking up of the earth's outer crust into plates. Most scientists, both creationists and evolutionists, agree that the continents we have today used to be all one landmass. However, they disagree on what caused the landmass to break apart. Many creationists believe this was part of the Flood. This breaking apart of the land led to massive volcanic activity and earth movements that resulted in the high mountain ranges we see today.

Also, the Flood caused major changes in the climate. It is believed that before

FUN FACT

Although the Bible gives us the true account of the Flood, many civilizations have flood stories as part of their history. For example, one of the oldest stories in existence is the *Epic of Gilgamesh*. This book contains a story of a man who built a boat that saved the lives of his family during a flood. The Chinese, Toltec, and Babylonian civilizations also have flood stories. In fact, there have been over 270 flood stories or records found around the world.

PICTURE OF THE ORIGINAL EARTH

Imagine what a world with no sin might have looked like. It would probably have been very green and lush, with no weeds or unpleasant plants. Genesis tells us that everything in Eden was watered by dew and underground springs. And there was no death. We know that God declared it "very good." Now draw a picture of what you think the earth might have looked like before the Fall.

the Flood, the climate was mostly tropical worldwide. After the Flood, it was much cooler, both because of cloud formation and because of increased ash in the air due to the volcanic activity. A cooler climate, along with more moisture from the Flood from warmer oceans, set up conditions that led to the Ice Age.

So most of what we see on the surface of the earth, and most of what we study in geology, is a direct result of God's judgment on the earth because of man's sin. Despite these judgments, the earth is still a magnificent place to live, and an exciting place to study. But it is amazing to realize how wonderful the earth must have been at creation, before the Fall, and before the Flood.

Someday we will experience God's completed plan for the earth. Revelation 21:1–2 says, "Now I saw a new heaven and a new earth, for the first heaven and the first earth had passed away. Also there was no more sea. Then I, John, saw the holy city, New Jerusalem, coming down out of heaven from God, prepared as a bride adorned for her husband." As we look forward to this, we can study the earth we have today and still see God's mighty hand in its design. ■

WHAT DID WE LEARN?

- What are some things geologists observe that point to a worldwide flood?

- What major geological events may have been associated with the Flood of Noah's day?

TAKING IT FURTHER

- How would a huge flood change the way the earth looks?

- Why did God send a huge flood?

DID THE FLOOD REALLY HAPPEN?

The Bible says that, "Scoffers will come in the last days, walking according to their own lusts, and saying, 'Where is the promise of His coming? For since the fathers fell asleep, all things continue as they were from the beginning of creation.' For this they willfully forget: that by the word of God the heavens were of old, and the earth standing out of water and in the water, by which the world that then existed perished, being flooded with water" (2 Peter 3:3–5). According to these verses, in the last days scoffers will choose to forget that God sent a worldwide flood and claim that things are continuing today as they always have. This seems to be what is happening in the minds of many people today. But is there any evidence for a worldwide flood? Complete the "Did the Flood Really Happen?" worksheet to find out.

THE SEARCH FOR NOAH'S ARK

Have you ever wanted to know where Noah's Ark landed and if it still exists today? The Bible says that it landed on the "mountains of Ararat." Most people believe this to be one of the mountains on the eastern border of Turkey. The mountain that is today called Mount Ararat is about 17,000 feet (5,180 m) tall. The ice at the top can be as much as 300 feet (91 m) thick. Because of the ice and the harsh weather, there are only two months out of the year when anyone can climb the mountain, and even then it is very difficult to climb. The mountain has frequent thunderstorms and is covered with deep crevasses in the ice that may be 200–300 feet (60–90 m) deep. This makes looking for the Ark very slow, difficult, and dangerous.

Another problem with looking for the Ark is that the Turkish government must approve any search, and only a few expeditions have been approved. Once approved, the search party has to be careful of the people who live on the mountain. Some explorers have been able to get protection from the Turkish army, but this requires even more work. Few groups have attempted the search, and no expeditions have been successful in proving that the Ark still exists today.

Despite these problems, there are several accounts of people who say they have seen the Ark in the past 150 years or so. One account occurred in 1856. Three English scientists went to Turkey and hired Haji Yearman and his father to help them find the Ark. The English-men were atheists who had come to prove there was no Ark. According to reports, however, upon finding the Ark the scientists threatened Haji and his father with persecution if they ever told anyone what they had found. Later, Haji became a Christian and moved to California. On his deathbed, he told his good friend, Harold Williams, about the Ark. A short time later, Mr. Williams read a newspaper account of an English scientist who confessed on his deathbed that as a young man, in 1856, he and two other scientists climbed Mt. Ararat and saw Noah's Ark.

In 1883, after some Turkish explorers claimed to have stumbled on the Ark, the Turkish government sent up a group of men to locate the Ark. They claim that after entering the Ark they deiced three compartments. They reported finding large cages, big enough to house very large animals. They also found what appeared to be the ship's log carved in an ancient language on the side of the third compartment. Could this have been Noah's Ark?

A story is told that in 1916, Lieutenant Roskovitsky of the Russian Imperial Air Force saw the Ark while flying over Mount Ararat. In 1939 *New Eden Magazine* quoted Roskovitsky as saying, "We flew down as close as safety permitted and took several circles around it. We were surprised when we got close to it, at the immense size of the thing, for it was as long as a city block, and would compare very favorably in size to the modern battleships of today. It was grounded on the shore of the lake, with one-fourth underwater. It had been partly dismantled on one side near the front, and on the other side there was a great doorway nearly twenty feet square . . . ."

Reportedly, this information was forwarded to the Russian tsar, who sent two engineering companies up the mountain. One group consisted of 50 people, and the other group consisted of 100 people. They said they found the Ark and measured and photographed it, and it compared closely to the sizes given in the Bible. The magazine article states that inside the Ark they found hundreds of small rooms and a few very large rooms with high ceilings. Other rooms had small cages along the walls with rows of small iron bars along the front of the cages. The craftsmanship showed a high level of design. The ship was made of Oleander wood. This wood belongs to the cypress family and resists rot. This type of wood, especially if it had been encased in ice most of the time since the Flood, could account for its near perfect preservation.

All the information was sent back to the tsar. But no one is sure what happened to this information. The expedition took place the same time as the Russian revolution of 1917. There are rumors that the pictures and information went to Leon Trotsky, who destroyed them and then killed the courier.

There have been other more recent sightings reported from the air. In 1960, Captain Gregor Schwinghammer and another pilot of the Turkish Air Force were on an observation flight around the mountain when Schwinghammer reported seeing "an enormous boxcar or rectangular barge visible in a gully high on the mountain." He stated that, "the Ark we saw was about 4,000 feet from the top (13,000 feet in altitude) on the southeast slope, perhaps four o'clock from due north."

In 1973 and 1976, two different high-

Mt. Ararat

powered intelligence-gathering satellites passed over the mountain and took some pictures. The photos supposedly show most of the anomaly trapped under the ice, with only the last section of it visible. The photos reportedly show a boat-like structure that is about 600 feet (180 m) long, but are of insufficient quality to make a certain identification.

But is it really important to find the Ark? If it does exist, it certainly would be a great archaeological find. However, we need to be careful because people tend to make such items into holy relics that are worshipped. The relic itself then almost takes the place of God in many instances. Christ actually taught that if people did not listen to "Moses and the prophets," then neither would something as spectacular as someone rising from the dead convince them (Luke 16). In other words, if people are not prepared to believe God's Word, finding Noah's Ark shouldn't be looked on as a priority to try and convince them.

It certainly would be exciting to find Noah's Ark, and maybe God will allow this to happen one day. In the meantime, we need to remember that our faith is not built on the finding of the Ark, but on the inerrant Word of the infallible Creator God. (For more information on Noah's Ark, visit www.answersingenesis.org/go/noah.)

The Great Ice Age

The age of woolly mammoths

LESSON

5

What caused the Ice Age and when did it occur?

Beginners

Before the Genesis Flood, the weather was warm over most of the earth, but after the Flood things were different. Many people believe that the continents were much cooler after the Flood due to the evaporation of warmer oceans causing more clouds, and because many volcanoes continued to erupt after the Flood, filling the sky with ash.

When more water evaporated from the warmer oceans it often resulted in snow, and a lot of snow fell in many areas. Because the weather inland was cool, this snow did not always melt and glaciers were formed. So much snow and ice formed in parts of the world that it was called the Ice Age.

During the Ice Age much of the northern and southern parts of the world was covered with ice, but the areas near the equator were still warm enough for people and animals to live and for plants to grow. Scientists do not all agree on how long the Ice Age lasted, but many creation scientists think it lasted for about 700 years. Eventually the ash settled and the oceans cooled, so less snow fell and more of the snow melted until the climate became much like it is today.

- How did the weather after the Flood compare to the weather before the Flood?
- What could make the weather cooler after the Flood?
- Was the earth completely covered with ice during the Ice Age?

Many areas of the earth show evidence of a great Ice Age, a time when much of the earth was covered with snow and glaciers. There is evidence that ice covered about 30% of the earth at one time, including northern Europe, all of Canada, much of the northern United States, and parts of New Zealand. There are areas of land that have been cut out by massive ice movements. And many specimens of animals, and even people, have been found encased in ice. Even mammoths (large hairy elephants) have been found encased in ice.

Evolutionists claim that slow climate changes have resulted in many cycles of a warm climate, followed by an ice age, followed by a warm climate. They believe that the most recent ice age started about 2 million years ago and ended about 11,000 years ago. Creationists believe there has only been one Ice Age and that the animal remains in the ice are only a few thousand years old. There is fossil evidence to support a much warmer, more tropical climate in the past, as well as evidence supporting a great Ice Age. However, evolutionists and creationists disagree on the age of these fossils and on the number of cycles that have occurred. Despite the disagreement about the dating methods and other evidence, scientists agree that for an ice age to form there must be two conditions: much wetter winters, resulting in large amounts of snowfall, and much cooler summers, preventing snow and ice from melting.

Scientists believe that the summers during an ice age would have been 20–40°F (11–17°C) cooler than they are today. They also believe that up to 80 feet (24 m) of snow would have fallen each year. At that rate, 40,000 feet (12,000 m) of snow could have fallen in 500 years. This would have compressed into 4,000 feet (1,200 m) of ice, resulting in massive glaciers. During this time people may have migrated from one area to another over land bridges that appeared because the sea level was lowered

During the Ice Age, nearly 30% of the land surface of the earth was covered by ice, which is identified in white. Today, only 10% of the earth's surface is covered by ice.

by all the ocean water now in the ice and snow on the continents. The uniformitarian idea of slow climatic changes suggested by evolutionists does not explain what would cause the temperatures to change and does not explain what would cause significantly more snowfall to occur at the same time.

On the other hand, the biblical account of the creation of the earth followed by a great Flood explains how a tropical climate was changed quickly into an ice age and eventually into the climate we see today. Prior to the Flood, the weather on the earth was much more uniform and warmer than today. During the Flood, the ocean waters were warmed by all the volcanic activity. After the Flood, conditions were just right for an ice age. The warmer oceans experienced much higher evaporation rates, resulting in large amounts of rain and snow. During the Flood there were massive volcanic eruptions, and volcanic activity continued after the Flood, spewing ash into the air, blocking some of the sunlight and causing much cooler temperatures over the entire earth, resulting in much cooler summers. These two conditions together would have resulted in an ice age. Eventually the ash settled, the waters in the oceans cooled, and the climate slowly warmed up and developed into the seasons that we have today. It is estimated that the Ice Age lasted about 700 years. (For more on the Ice Age, visit www.answersingenesis.org/go/ice-age.) ■

ICE AGE CROSSWORD PUZZLE

Test your understanding of the climate conditions during the Ice Age by completing the "Ice Age Crossword Puzzle."

WHAT DID WE LEARN?

- What two conditions are necessary for an ice age?
- How did the Genesis Flood set up conditions for the Ice Age?
- How do evolutionists explain the needed conditions for multiple ice ages?

TAKING IT FURTHER

- Do we see new glaciers forming today?

ICE AGE IDEAS

There are several evolutionary ideas that try to explain how ice ages happen. One idea is based on the current idea that increased carbon dioxide could lead to global warming so decreased carbon dioxide in the atmosphere could lead to global cooling. However, there is no known mechanism for decreasing the carbon dioxide in the atmosphere and even if there was, this would likely only lower the temperature by a few degrees, not enough for an ice age.

Other scientists claim that the increased temperatures from global warming will affect the flow of warmer water in the North Atlantic, causing northern Europe to become colder and possibly triggering a future ice age. However, this flow has decreased by 30% in the past 50 years and has caused no noticeable change in the earth's climate.

Another idea is called the astronomical theory. The earth's orbit around the sun is an ellipse or a slightly flattened circle. The shape of the earth's orbit varies slightly over time. This changes the amount of sunlight falling on the earth. However, the amount of sunlight changes by only 0.17% at the most so this cannot account for the changes needed to bring on an ice age. Although the decrease in sunlight might make a difference of one or two degrees, it could not make the required difference of 20 to 40 degrees needed to bring about an ice age.

These ideas only account for changes in temperature and do not explain where the increased moisture and evaporation might come from. The Bible explains why there would have been greater evaporation after the Flood. Genesis 7:11 tells us that when the Flood began, "the fountains of the great deep burst forth." This means that water from under the ground burst out of the ground. The water under the surface of the earth is often much hotter than surface water. All you have to do is go to Yellowstone National Park and watch the geysers erupting to see how hot water can shoot out of the ground. This hot water, mixing with the rainwater would have greatly increased the temperature of the oceans, thus allowing for greater evaporation rates than we see today. The water would have condensed as snow and ice over the cooler continents. Since the summers were cooler, the snow didn't melt and the ice sheets continued to grow.

Purpose: To understand the extent of the Ice Age

Materials: world map, climate map, crayons or markers

Procedure:

1. Get a copy of a climate map of the world that shows areas that are currently covered with ice.

2. On a world map color these areas dark green. This will include most of Greenland and the northernmost parts of Canada, Antarctica, as well as parts of Siberia.

3. Next, color the additional areas that were covered with ice during the Ice Age in light green. This would include Iceland, all of Canada, most of Alaska, and part of the United States including New England, Minnesota, Iowa, Illinois, Indiana, Ohio, and Pennsylvania, as well as some of the higher mountains from Colorado to California. It would also include southern parts of New Zealand and the southernmost tip of South America.

4. Make a key for your map showing what each color represents.

Conclusion: The middle and southern parts of the United States, Mexico, Central America, South America, as well as southern Europe, most of Asia, the Middle East, and most of Africa and Australia were still habitable during the Ice Age, though they would have been cooler and wetter than they are today.

GLACIERS

Ice that never melts

LESSON

6

What are the types of glaciers and where are they found?

Words to know:

zone of wastage

zone of accumulation

valley glacier

piedmont glacier

continental glacier

calving

BEGINNERS

Glaciers are sheets of ice that never completely melt. In areas where glaciers exist, snow falls during the winter; during the summer some, but not all, of the snow melts. The next winter, more snow falls and the weight of the new snow presses the older snow down, turning it into ice. Many of the glaciers that exist today are left over from the Ice Age, but others are new glaciers.

When a glacier forms on top of a mountain, gravity pulls down on it and the ice moves down into the valleys. Other glaciers form in flat areas and spread out in all directions. These relatively flat glaciers are found in Greenland and Antarctica. Most glaciers today are found near the North and South poles.

Sometimes glaciers move past the edge of land and reach the water. When this happens chunks of the glacier break off. Ice is lighter than water so these chunks float in the water. These floating chunks of ice are called icebergs. Icebergs can be very large. When they are large, most of the iceberg stays below the surface of the water and only a small part can be seen above the water. This can be a very dangerous situation for ships that are sailing in icy waters. In 1912 the Titanic, a large ship, hit an iceberg and sank.

- **What is a glacier?**

- **Where are most glaciers located?**

- **Where do icebergs come from?**

Most glaciers that formed during the Ice Age have melted, but some have just receded, and in a few areas, new glaciers continue to form and grow. Glaciers are thick sheets of ice that form in areas where summers are cool enough that the winter snows do not completely melt, and snow accumulates year after year. The weight of accumulated snow compacts the snow below it, forming it into ice.

An area where snow falls but does not completely melt is called a snowfield. Snow will melt and evaporate in the lower part of the snowfield, but snow that falls above the "snow line" does not melt and accumulates year after year. The area where snow melts is called the **zone of wastage**, and the area where the snow accumulates is called the **zone of accumulation**.

As the weight of the snow and ice increases, the effects of gravity become apparent. Gravity pulls the ice down any slope. The greater or steeper the slope, the more the ice moves down it. A glacier that spreads down a valley is called a **valley glacier**. If two or more glaciers move down nearby valleys and combine and spread out into a more flat area, they form a **piedmont glacier**.

However, more than 95% of the ice in glaciers is not in the form of valley or piedmont glaciers, but in the form of giant ice sheets called continental glaciers. These continental glaciers are mostly in Antarctica and Greenland. An ice sheet, or **continental glacier**, is a glacier in a relatively flat area that spreads out in all directions rather than flowing downhill.

Most glaciers today are found at or near the North and South poles and on very high mountain peaks. These regions remain cold even in the summer so the ice does

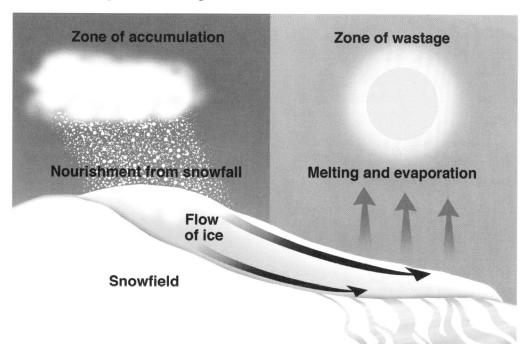

ICEBERG DANGER

Purpose: To understand the danger of icebergs

Materials: bowl, ice cubes, toy boat

Procedure:

1. Fill a bowl about half full of water.

2. Add several ice cubes. Notice how much of the ice cube is above the surface and how much is below.

3. Take a toy boat and try to steer it through the icebergs without hitting them.

Conclusion: How fast can you steer the boat when there are lots of ice cubes? This demonstrates the dangers that icebergs pose to ships.

not completely melt. Today, ice covers about 10% of the earth's surface. The world's largest glacier is on Antarctica and covers about 5.5 million square miles (14 million square km).

As glaciers move to the edge of land, they reach water. Ice is lighter than (less dense than) water so the edge of the glacier begins to float. Eventually this upward pressure causes some of the ice to break off of the glacier and fall into the water. This process is called **calving**. The pieces of ice that break off a glacier into the water become icebergs (shown below). Icebergs often move out into the open ocean and can become very dangerous to ships. Only a small portion of the iceberg is visible above the surface of the water and the unexposed portion poses a significant danger. The most famous disaster caused by an iceberg is the sinking of the *Titanic* in 1912. ■

FUN FACT

A major section of ice may be close to calving from Antarctica. If this happens, it will change the coastline enough to require changes in most maps.

FUN FACT

One of the largest icebergs ever measured was 208 miles (335 km) long and 62 miles (100 km) wide. That's bigger than the state of Massachusetts!

WHAT DID WE LEARN?

- What is a glacier?
- How does a glacier form?
- What are the three types of glaciers?
- What is calving?

TAKING IT FURTHER

- Why do glaciers exist mostly at the poles and on high mountain tops?
- Why is it cold enough to prevent glaciers from melting at the North pole, when there is 20–24 hours of sunlight during the summer?

CHANGING TEMPERATURES

Glaciers experience cycles of growth and retreat depending on climate conditions. Currently most glaciers in the world are retreating; they are becoming smaller each year. However, in the past there have been extensive periods of glacier growth.

From approximately 1450 to 1850 was a period that has been dubbed the Little Ice Age. During this time period there are records that the glaciers around the world advanced nearly every year. Villages in northern Europe were destroyed by the advancing ice, and many people had to move to lower elevations. It is believed that the Vikings abandoned their homes in Greenland and Iceland and moved to other areas.

The climate change caused cooler temperatures and resulted in shorter growing seasons in many parts of Europe and North America. Rivers that normally do not freeze are recorded to have frozen many times during this time period. A famous example in America is seen in the painting of George Washington crossing the Delaware River amidst flowing ice. Today the Delaware River seldom freezes. Shorter growing seasons led to increased famine and many people died as a result.

So what caused this Little Ice Age? The exact causes are unknown, but scientists believe that there were two main factors that contributed to the colder temperatures. First, there was very little sunspot activity and the sunlight was less intense. Also, there was an increase in volcanic activity adding a significant amount of ash to the air. These two conditions combined to create a colder climate for several hundred years.

Since about 1850, temperatures have increased and growing seasons have lengthened. Glaciers have retreated in many areas. Some people see this as a natural rebound from the Little Ice Age due to reduced volcanic activity and increased solar output. However, other scientists see this as a precursor to catastrophic global warming.

The truth is that scientists don't really know how much of the warming effect is natural and how much is caused by industrialization. The actual increase in temperature over the past 100 years is about 1.2 degrees Fahrenheit (0.67 degrees Celsius). About half of this is likely to be caused by natural changes in the climate. Thus, the temperature increase due to increased carbon dioxide levels is really only about 0.6°F (0.34°C). More research is needed to really determine how much man can affect the climate and how much change is just natural cycles in temperature.

SIR ERNEST SHACKLETON & THE *ENDURANCE*

Imagine what it would be like to be trapped in the ice floes around the South Pole. Imagine what it would be like to endure day after day of total darkness in temperatures down to 100 degrees below zero. Imagine what it would be like to have the ice under your feet suddenly split and break in two. This, and much more, happened to 28 men on an expedition to the South pole in 1914.

Sir Ernest Shackleton, captain of the ship *Endurance*, along with 27 other men, sailed from England on August 8, 1914, the same day that World War I began. Their goal was to be the first men to cross Antarctica on foot. They took dogs and sleds to carry their supplies, and loaded the *Endurance* with food and equipment for the dangerous journey.

They traveled south into the freezing waters of the South Atlantic. While they were still nearly 100 miles (160 km) from their landing site, the *Endurance* became trapped in the ice

floes and they were unable to break free. From January–October 1915, the crew lived onboard the ship, each day hoping to see a break in the ice so they could continue their journey. But the ice just closed in tighter around them.

During this time, the crew experienced their first polar winter. Weeks passed with no sunlight. It was an endless darkness that troubled the minds of many of the men. In addition, the temperatures were very cold—often down to −100ºF (−73ºC).

After nearly nine months of being trapped in the ice, the pressure became too great and the ship succumbed to the ice and began to break apart. The men were forced to abandon the ship, saving what they could, and began living on the ice floes. Because of the movement of the ocean, the ice floes were not stable. Even very large pieces of ice, some a mile wide, would suddenly crack and split apart. Several times the men had to break camp with little notice and move to another piece of ice as the one they had been on broke apart.

The men were able to save much of their supplies along with three small boats, which they began to try to move across the ice using the dogs and sleds. This proved to be extremely difficult. And after only a few days of exhausting work, they had made very little progress toward land. They decided to let the movement of the ice take them closer to land.

After months of living on the boat and weeks of living on the ice, the food supplies became very low. They were able to survive by hunting seals and penguins and by using seal blubber for fuel. However, eventually they were forced to shoot their dogs because there was no food for the dogs. This saddened the men.

Finally, after nearly six months of living in the open, moving from ice floe to ice floe, there was enough of an opening in the ice that they were able to launch the three small boats. They were able to sail these boats between ice floes to the last island within nearly 1,000 miles (1,600 km). The island was called Elephant Island and was little more than a desolate rock. However, it was solid ground and did not split unexpectedly with the shifting of the ice. After 497 days, the crew was on solid ground again.

It was decided that the best chance they had for rescue was for six men to take one of the three open boats and try to row to the nearest inhabited land which was over 800 miles (1,285 km) away. Shackleton and five other men set sail on April 24, 1916, on a course for South Georgia Island where they hoped to get help from whalers that worked there that time of year.

On May 10, 1916, against incredible odds, Shackleton and his men reached South Georgia Island. They landed on the west side of the island and were unable to sail around the island due to bad weather. So three of the men decided to climb the giant mountains of ice to reach the whalers' camp. When they finally reached the camp, they were received as if they had risen from the dead. Despite the incredible hardship he had endured, Shackleton rested for only one day before setting out to rescue the rest of his crew.

Over the next three months, Ernest Shackleton used every resource he had to obtain ships to try to sail back to Elephant Island. Every attempt was met with defeat. Several times ships had to turn back because of the ice. A ship that was able to withstand the ice was sent from England but would take weeks to arrive. Shackleton was unwilling to wait and kept looking for another way to rescue his crew. Finally, Shackleton was able to borrow a ship from the Chilean government, and the weather cooperated long enough for them to reach Elephant Island on August 30, 1916, more than four months after he had left his crew there.

Amazingly, every man that set out on the expedition in August 1914 was rescued in August 1916. The amazing stamina and hope of these men and their trust in their captain is a story that should not be forgotten. After being rescued, every man said that he felt that there was a supernatural being that was watching over him. They all felt the presence of God throughout their amazing ordeal. Ernest Shackleton said in a speech in 1920, "I have no doubt that Providence guided us, not only across the snowfields, but across the storm-white sea that separated Elephant Island from our landing place on South Georgia. I know that during that long and racking march of thirty-six hours over the unnamed mountains and glaciers of South Georgia, it seemed to me often that we were four, not three."

To learn more about this amazing adventure and the bravery of these men, read *Endurance: Shackleton's Incredible Voyage* by Alfred Lansing.

MOVEMENT OF GLACIERS

Slowly creeping down the valley

LESSON
7

How does a glacier move and what features does it create?

Words to know:

striations

terminal moraine

lateral moraine

glacial erratic

BEGINNERS

Glaciers are large sheets of ice. Gravity pulls on these sheets of ice and causes them to move. The bottom layers of the ice are more flexible than the top layers of ice, so they move more easily than the top layers. This can cause the top layers to get large cracks in them.

When the ice moves, it drags rocks, dirt, and other debris with it. When the weather is warm, the ice begins to melt and the water flows into the soil and rocks under the glacier. When it becomes cold again, this water freezes and the rocks and other debris become frozen in the ice. When the ice is pulled down a hill by gravity, the rocks in the ice act like sandpaper and scrape the ground and rocks underneath it.

Glaciers also push rocks and dirt ahead of them. Then, when the glacier begins to melt, it leaves a line of rocks showing where the ice has been. Glaciers usually move very slowly, only a few inches each day.

• What makes a glacier move?

• What moves along with the ice?

• How can you tell how far a glacier has moved in the past?

A glacier is a sheet or river of moving ice. This movement is caused by gravity. But the glacier doesn't necessarily move as one solid piece. The lower layer of ice is moldable and takes on the shape of the terrain over which it flows. This lower layer flows on a melted layer of water. However, upper layers of ice are not as compressed and are more brittle. The upper layers cannot move smoothly like the lower layers and often crack, sometimes forming huge crevasses.

Although the lower layers are moldable, the movement of the glacier does considerable damage to the terrain over which it moves. Glacier movement is nearly unstoppable due to the great mass of ice, and it levels nearly everything in its path. Glaciers dig out the sides of the valleys through which they pass, giving them a U-shaped appearance instead of the usual V-shaped appearance of most valleys.

As the edges of a glacier melt and then refreeze, the ice picks up rocks and debris that get added to the glacier. This debris acts like sandpaper on the underside of the glacier and scratches lines, called striations, into the ground over which it flows.

Glaciers also push rocks and debris ahead of their advance. Once the glacier quits advancing, the line of rocks that is left behind marks the furthest advance of the

FUN FACT

In general, glaciers only move a few inches per day. But sometimes they move very rapidly. One glacier on an island north of Norway averaged 60 feet (18 m) per day for three years. The fastest moving glacier ever recorded was the Kutiah Glacier, north of India, that moved 7.5 miles (12 km) in three months.

MAKING A MINI-GLACIER

Purpose: To observe how a glacier changes the terrain over which it flows

Materials: sand, pebbles, half-gallon milk carton, gloves

Procedure:

1. Place a handful of sand and a handful of pebbles into an empty half-gallon milk carton.

2. Fill the carton with water to within two inches of the top.

3. Place the carton in the freezer and freeze overnight.

4. When the water is frozen, remove it from the carton. Now you have a "mini-glacier."

5. Put on a pair of gloves and take the glacier to a hill. A hill with soft dirt and a gentle slope is best.

6. Place the ice at the top of the hill with the edge having the most visible sand and pebbles facing down. Then, while pressing down hard, slowly slide the ice down the hill for several feet. Notice the changes in the hill.

7. Leave the ice where it is and allow it to melt. After the ice is completely melted, look at the area where the ice had been.

Questions:

- How did the movement of the ice affect the surface of the hill?

- Can you see striations—lines made in the dirt by the sand and pebbles in the ice?

- Is there a line of dirt and rocks at the front edge of the glacier?

- What did you see after the ice melted? Is there an area of pebbles that moved with the glacier?

Conclusion: All of the features you noticed are similar to the features that glaciers make. Glaciers scrape the ground as they move and often leave behind rocks and dirt when they melt.

glacier. This line of rocks is called the **terminal moraine**. Rocks and debris are also pushed up along the sides of the glacier and are called **lateral moraines**.

Sometimes, glaciers move huge boulders as they advance. Once they begin to melt, they often leave a path of large rocks and boulders behind. Some of these rocks have been carried miles away from where they originated. An enormous boulder deposited by a glacier is called a **glacial erratic**. ■

WHAT DID WE LEARN?

- What is the shape of a valley carved by glaciers?
- How do glaciers pick up rocks and other debris?
- What is the name of the line of rocks that marks the furthest advance of the glacier?

TAKING IT FURTHER

- How might a scientist tell how far a glacier moved a rock or boulder?
- Why do glaciers often have deep cracks and crevasses?

THE FORCE OF WATER

As glaciers move, they greatly change the way the ground underneath the ice looks. Glacier ice melts and freezes over and over again. As the water moves into cracks in rocks and then freezes, the water expands and causes the rock to crack. Eventually, pieces of rock break off and become part of the glacier. These pieces of rock can be moved miles away from their original location. Eventually, when the glacier retreats, areas where the glacier has been look very different from how they looked before the glacier passed over them. One example of this is the Matterhorn (pictured here), one of the most famous mountains in Switzerland. It is believed that two glaciers met at this spot and both broke off large sections of the rock face, leaving behind a very pointed peak.

Purpose: To see the unyielding force of freezing water

Materials: glass jar with lid, newspaper, zipper bag, freezer, work gloves

Procedure:

1. Fill a glass jar completely with water and put the lid on tightly.

2. Wrap the jar in several layers of newspaper, place it in a plastic zipper bag, and seal the bag.

3. Place the bag in the freezer and allow the water to freeze overnight.

4. After the water has frozen, remove the bag from the freezer.

5. Using work gloves, very carefully remove the jar from the bag and slowly unwrap the paper.

Questions: What happened to the jar filled with water? Why did this happen?

Conclusion: You will see that the water has broken the glass or has pushed off the top. Water expands when it freezes, and this experiment illustrates how freezing water can break rock. It may not seem that water alone could cause such devastation to a huge mountain like the Matterhorn, but over time it is possible. Glaciers are not the only place that we see freezing water causing things to break apart. Sidewalks can get cracks that expand with freezing water. Streets can also experience this problem. Water can be an unstoppable force. **(Be sure to carefully dispose of any broken glass in a safe container.)**

UNIT 2

ROCKS & MINERALS

◊ **Describe** the basic structure of the earth.

◊ **Describe** how each of the three types of rocks is formed.

◊ **Identify** the conditions required for fossilization.

◊ **Describe** the formation of fossil fuels.

◊ **Explain** why minerals are important to mankind.

DESIGN OF THE EARTH

Blueprint for the planet

What is the earth like on the inside?

Words to know:

crust

mantle

core

BEGINNERS

Scientists use instruments to help them figure out what is inside the earth. These instruments measure earthquake waves that move under the surface. The information from these waves causes scientists to believe that the earth has three main parts: the crust, the mantle, and the core. The crust is the outside of the earth. This is the only part of the earth that we ever see. The **crust** is made of rock and is the thinnest of the three parts of the planet.

Underneath the crust is the mantle. The **mantle** is the thickest part of the earth. The mantle is very hot compared to the surface of the earth. It is so hot inside the mantle that rocks can melt. Melted rocks inside the earth are called magma.

In the center of the earth is the **core**. Scientists are not sure what the core is made of, but they know it is very hot. They believe that it is so hot and under so much pressure that it is a solid ball of metal (even though it is hotter than the mantle).

- What are the three parts of the earth?

- What is the hottest part of the earth?

- What is the thinnest part of the earth?

How did God design this ball we call earth? How can scientists know what is inside without actually seeing it? Most of the information that we have about the interior of the earth has been obtained by studying how earthquake waves travel through the earth. Seismic waves travel at different speeds through different types of material. By studying how the waves move through the earth, scientists can make predictions about what the interior of the earth is like. There are over a million earthquakes, mostly minor, each year that scientists track to help them study the earth. Based on these observations, scientists believe that the earth is composed of three main layers: the crust, the mantle, and the core.

The **crust** is the outermost part of the earth. It is made of solid rock and is between 3 and 37 miles (5–60 km) thick. The thickest parts of the crust are under the mountain ranges, and the thinnest parts are under the oceans. The crust is the only layer of the earth that we can directly observe. Even though several projects have attempted to drill deeply into the crust, none has ever reached the mantle. The costs and heat are too great to drill to the mantle.

In 1909 Andrija Mohorovicic (mo-ho-ro-VEECH-itch) discovered that seismic waves change speed below the crust. The area where this change occurs has been named the Mohorovicic Discontinuity or Moho for short. The Moho is the boundary between the earth's crust and the **mantle**. Scientists believe the mantle is approximately 1,800 miles (2,900 km) thick and comprises about 84% of the earth's volume. It is hotter and denser than the crust, so seismic waves travel more quickly through the mantle than through the crust. The top of the mantle is semi-rigid. The lower part of the mantle moves slowly with convection currents, which means that as the hotter magma rises toward the surface, the cooler magma falls toward the center of the earth.

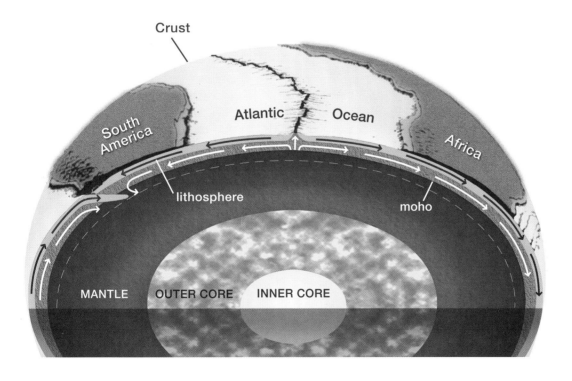

MAKING A MODEL OF THE EARTH

Purpose: To make a fun (and delicious) model of the earth

Materials: marshmallow, gumball, chocolate chips, bowl, wax paper, toothpick

Procedure:

1. Take a large marshmallow and carefully cut a small slit in one side.

2. Insert a gumball. The gumball represents the core, and the marshmallow represents the mantle.

3. Melt some chocolate chips in a microwave-safe bowl.

4. Using a toothpick, carefully dip the marshmallow into the melted chocolate. The chocolate represents the earth's crust.

5. Set your model on waxed paper to cool. After the chocolate has set, review the parts of the earth, and then eat your yummy model!

SEISMIC WAVES

Purpose: To better understand how seismic waves give scientists a picture of what is under the earth's crust

Materials: serving bowl, bottle or jar, pencil

Procedure:

1. Fill a serving bowl half full of water.

2. Place a bottle or jar in the center of the bowl.

3. Gently tap the surface of the water near the edge of the bowl with the end of a pencil and carefully observe the direction and speed of the waves as they travel across the surface of the water.

Conclusion: The waves bounce off of the bottle and travel back toward the edge of the bowl. Similarly, some seismic waves travel through liquids and bounce off of solid objects, while others travel through solid objects and are reflected off of liquids. These various waves help scientists get a better understanding of the interior of the earth.

The top part of the mantle, together with the crust, is called the lithosphere. The lithosphere is believed to float on the more fluid inner mantle. Instead of being one solid piece of rock, the lithosphere is believed to be broken into 13 plates that move independently of one another.

The innermost part of the earth is the core. It accounts for about 15% of the total volume of the earth. The actual composition of the core is unknown and some geologists refuse to even guess what it might be like. Others believe the core to be extremely hot and dense. The most widely accepted model splits the core into two parts. The outer core is believed to be liquid metal about 1,400 miles (2,250 km) thick. The inner core is believed to be a solid metal ball with a radius of about 800 miles (1,290 km). The inner core is thought to be under so much pressure that it can't melt despite the belief that its temperature may be as much as 13,000°F (7,200°C). Because the earth has a magnetic field, it is thought that the core must be mostly iron or iron and nickel. ■

EARTH'S COMPOSITION

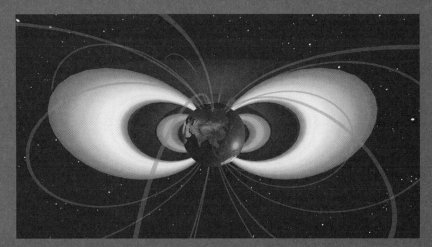

Although scientists are not sure what the core of the earth is made of, most believe that it is probably made from iron and nickel. This idea is based mostly on the fact that the earth has a large magnetic field surrounding it. In 1958, a scientist named James Van Allen proved that there was an area around the earth that contains a high amount of radiation. It was later shown that there are two areas reaching hundreds of miles into space that trap radiation due to a large magnetic field generated by the earth (see illustration).

The best explanation that scientists have come up with for how the magnetic field is generated is that current is flowing through the core of the earth. Thus, if the core is made of a magnetic material such as iron or nickel, this current would produce a magnetic field—essentially turning the earth into a giant electromagnet. Because of this magnetic field, many

scientists believe the core must be made of mostly iron or iron and nickel.

In reality, scientists know very little about the core or the mantle. They know much more about the crust. Although the earth's crust contains 92 known elements, only 8 elements are found in abundance. About 47% of the earth's crust contains oxygen. This does not mean that the crust contains oxygen gas; rather, the oxygen is bonded with other elements to form the

oxide rocks that make up the crust. The second most common element in the earth's crust is silicon, comprising approximately 28% of the crust by weight. Silicon is also bonded with many other elements to form the silicate rocks found in the crust. Aluminum makes up about 8%, iron makes up about 5%, and calcium, sodium, potassium, and magnesium each make up from 2–4% of the crust. The other 84 elements together comprise only 1.4% of the earth's crust.

Activity 1—Purpose: To make a pie chart showing which elements are found in the earth's crust

Materials: piece of paper, protractor, pencil

Procedure:

1. Draw a circle on a blank piece of paper.

2. Using a protractor, from the center of the circle draw a 169 degree angle and label this piece of the pie *Oxygen*. This is 47% of the circle.

3. From one side of this angle draw a 101 degree angle and label this piece *Silicon*.

4. Continue by drawing a 29 degree angle for *Aluminum* and an 18 degree angle for *Iron*.

5. The rest of the pie, approximately 46 degrees or 12%, can be labeled as *Other*.

6. Be sure to label your chart "Elements in the Earth's Crust."

Activity 2—Purpose: To visualize how magma cools to form crust

Materials: ¼ cup chocolate chips, bowl, zipper bag, cup

Procedure:

1. Melt ¼ cup chocolate chips in the microwave. Do not overheat them.

2. Pour this liquid chocolate into a plastic zipper bag.

3. Fill a cup with cold water.

4. Cut a small corner from the plastic bag and squeeze the liquid chocolate into the cold water.

Conclusion:

The earth's crust has been classified into two different parts: the continental crust and the oceanic crust. The continental crust is the part of the land that is not part of the ocean basins. Most continental crust is composed of granite covered with sedimentary rock. The ocean basin, or oceanic crust, is composed mostly of basalt, which is a darker and denser rock than granite. In your experiment you saw how the liquid quickly cooled and became a solid. This is similar to how liquid magma cools and solidifies as it enters the oceans. It is believed that the ocean basins were formed as magma squeezed up from below the crust and solidified as it was cooled by the water.

ROCKS

Boulders, rocks, gravel, pebbles . . .

LESSON

9

What are rocks made of and how are they formed?

Words to know:

igneous

sedimentary

metamorphic

Challenge words:

vesicles

BEGINNERS

Rocks are always underneath you. Even when you are swimming in a lake or the ocean, there are rocks below the water and sand. If you dig down below the dirt, you will eventually hit rock. These rocks form the crust of the earth.

There are three kinds of rocks. **Igneous** rocks were formed when liquid rock from under the crust cooled as it came out of the inside of the earth. **Sedimentary** rocks were formed as bits and pieces of sand and broken rocks were glued together to form new rock. The third kind of rock is metamorphic rock. **Metamorphic** rock is igneous or sedimentary rock that has changed into another kind of rock because of heat and pressure.

We will learn more about each of these kinds of rocks in the next several lessons. Later in this book you will be making a rock collection, so start looking for interesting rocks and save them for your collection.

• Where can you find rocks?

• What are the three different kinds of rocks?

Igneous

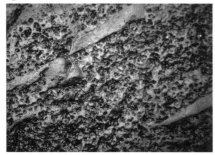

Sedimentary

Metamorphic

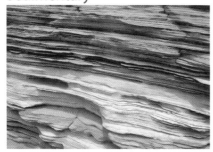

Whether you realize it or not, rock is always underneath you. Even when you are swimming in a lake or walking on a beach, even if you are mowing the grass or hiking through the forest, if you dig down deep enough, you will hit solid rock. This rock is the crust of the earth. Many of the rocks that we pick up are just small pieces that have broken off of the crust.

Rocks are very important to our lives. Rocks are the foundations on which we build our buildings, and the materials with which we build many structures. Coal is an important source of fuel. And rocks add beauty to our lives.

Rocks are a combination of one or more minerals or organic materials. A few rocks contain only one mineral, but most are a combination of two or more minerals. Scientists group rocks into three categories by how they are formed. **Igneous** rocks are formed when melted minerals, called magma, cool and harden. **Sedimentary** rocks are formed when layers of sediment are pressed and "cemented" together. The third type, **metamorphic** rocks, are formed when igneous or sedimentary rocks are exposed to pressure and heat. Over time, they are changed into different rocks with different atomic structures.

Rocks are not only important for buildings and monuments, they are very important for growing plants. Soil is made from ground up bits of rocks mixed with clay, dead leaves, sticks, and small pebbles. It is important to have rocks around to make new soil.

People who like to collect and study rocks are often nicknamed *rock hounds*. For the final project in lesson 34, you will become a rock hound. So begin looking for interesting rocks to add to your collection. You will enjoy learning about rocks. ■

ROCK CYCLE WORKSHEET

All rock on earth was formed at Creation. Yet much of that rock has been recycled into other types of rock. All three types of rock can be melted to form magma. This magma can then be cooled and will solidify to form new igneous rock. Also, all three types of rock can be broken into tiny bits by weathering. Bits of sediment eventually settle and are pressed together and cemented to form new sedimentary rock. And finally, both sedimentary and igneous rock can be changed by pressure, heat, and time into various types of metamorphic rock.

Label and color the "Rock Cycle" worksheet.

WHAT DID WE LEARN?

- What are rocks made from?
- What are the three categories of rocks?
- How is igneous rock formed?
- How is sedimentary rock formed?
- How is metamorphic rock formed?

TAKING IT FURTHER

- Why are rocks important?
- Where is a good place to look for rocks?
- Why is it better to store your rock samples in a box with dividers than in a bag?

IDENTIFYING ROCKS

There are three kinds of rocks: igneous, sedimentary, and metamorphic. If you pick up a rock from the ground, how can you tell which kind of rock it is? There are many tests that can be done to determine the exact type of rock or mineral you may have; however, there are a few common characteristics that will be helpful in making a quick determination of the type of rock.

Igneous rocks have an interlocking grain texture. You will see this clearly when looking at a sample of granite. Sometimes these grains may be of two very different sizes. Often igneous rocks have holes called **vesicles**. Rocks with many holes are sometimes called lava rock (shown here). Many igneous rocks have a dark color and are heavy.

Sedimentary rocks have small pieces that are cemented together, so if you can easily rub part of the rock off with your finger it is almost certainly a sedimentary rock. Sandstone is an obvious example of a sedimentary rock. If the rock looks like small rocks all glued together, then it is a sedimentary rock. Also, only sedimentary rocks contain recognizable fossils. Often sedimentary rocks are light colored and lightweight.

Metamorphic rocks at first glance may appear to be igneous or sedimentary rocks, but have some distinct differences. Metamorphic rocks usually have foliation or layering. Also, they often have bands of light and dark colors. They can have a large grain texture. And if you tap a metamorphic rock it will sound more like a *ching*, whereas other rocks have more of a *chunk* sound.

Now that you have an idea of what to look for, select a few rock samples that you find outside or may have around your house and see if you can determine which are igneous, which are sedimentary, and which are metamorphic. You don't need to identify exactly what kind of rocks you have, just what category each fits into.

IGNEOUS ROCKS

Fire rocks

LESSON 10

How are igneous rocks formed?

Words to know:

magma

lava

extrusive

intrusive

Challenge words:

porphyritic

BEGINNERS

Have you ever seen pictures of a volcano? The fiery red liquid coming out of the volcano is lava. **Lava** is liquid rock that has come to the surface of the earth's crust. The rock has become a liquid because it was heated so much underground that it melted. When the liquid rock is still inside the earth it is called **magma**. When liquid rock cools down it forms igneous rocks.

The magma can cool while it is still in the ground. Because it is hotter inside the earth, the magma cools very slowly. This allows crystals to grow as the rocks form. So some igneous rocks have large crystals in them.

Sometimes the lava shoots out of the ground. Then the melted rock cools very quickly and does not have time to form crystals. These new rocks are also igneous rocks, but they look different from the rocks that are formed inside the earth's crust.

One kind of common igneous rock is called granite. You have probably seen granite used to make monuments and statues. Another common igneous rock is called obsidian. Obsidian is very shiny and usually black. It is often used to make arrowheads.

- How is igneous rock formed?

- Do crystals grow in rocks that formed inside the earth or on top of the earth?

- What are two uses for igneous rocks?

Igneous is the Latin word for *fire* and thus igneous rocks are fire rocks. These rocks are formed when molten or melted rock cools and hardens into new rock. This melted rock is called magma when it is below the earth's surface and is called lava once it emerges from the earth's crust. Igneous rocks can form both inside the earth's crust and on the earth's surface.

Rocks that form on the earth's surface are called extrusive rocks and are often nicknamed "lava rocks." Extrusive rocks cool quickly and therefore do not have time to form large crystals. They usually have very small crystals or no crystals at all. Pumice is a common extrusive igneous rock. It is light colored and full of holes because it cooled when the lava was full of hot gases. Because it cooled quickly, the gases were trapped inside. Eventually the gases escaped, leaving the holes behind. These air bubbles make pumice very light, and samples can often float on the water. Basalt is a heavy lava rock that occurs throughout the world. Obsidian, often called natural glass, is an igneous rock that cooled very quickly and has no crystals at all. However, it is often very shiny and thus looks like colored glass. Common colors for obsidian are black, brown, and red. It was often used to make arrowheads, like the one shown here.

Intrusive rocks are igneous rocks that were formed inside the earth's crust. Magma may flow away from the area where it was heated to a cooler area inside the earth's crust. Because these rocks formed where the temperatures were much higher than on the surface, they cooled much more slowly, allowing crystals to grow much larger. The most common intrusive rock is granite. Granite is a mixture of quartz, feldspar, and mica. It is easy to see these three minerals in the granite shown to the right. The mica is usually black, the feldspar is pink, and the quartz is white. Granite is very strong and withstands weathering so it is often used for buildings and monuments. The Vietnam Veterans Memorial in Washington, D.C. is made from black granite.

Sometimes intrusive rocks form with larger crystals embedded in smaller crystals. What most likely happened to cause this was that the magma was in a warm area and the larger crystals formed, then somehow the magma was shifted to a cooler area and cooled more quickly allowing only small crystals to form.

FUN FACT

Devils Tower in Wyoming is the remains of a volcano. The magma inside the neck of the volcano hardened after the volcano became inactive. Eventually, the soil above it wore away, leaving a giant tower of igneous rock.

GROWING CRYSTALS

Purpose: To show what factors determine crystal size and shape

Materials: saucepan, stove, alum, two cups, craft stick, refrigerator

Procedure:

1. Place one cup of water in a saucepan and slowly heat it over medium heat until boiling.

2. Carefully add alum to the water until no more will dissolve or until you have dissolved about 2 ounces of alum.

3. Carefully pour half of the alum water into each of two cups.

4. Place a craft stick into each cup and put one cup in the refrigerator where it will not be disturbed for several days, and put the second cup in a location at room temperature where it will not be disturbed for several days.

5. Observe the contents of each cup every day for several days. After several days, crystals should be growing in both cups.

Questions:

- How do the crystals that formed in the refrigerator compare to those that formed at room temperature? Are the crystals the same shape? Are they the same size? Were they made of the same material?

- Why do they look so different?

Conclusion: The cup in the refrigerator will demonstrate the formation of extrusive rocks—rocks that cool quickly—and should have crystals that are smaller. The cup at room temperature will demonstrate the formation of intrusive rocks—rocks that cool slowly—and should have larger crystals. Since they both contain the same mineral, the shape of the crystals will be the same.

Igneous rocks are a part of our lives everyday. From monuments to counter tops, igneous rocks are all around us. One man-made rock that is used nearly everywhere is concrete. Concrete is made from cement, which contains volcanic ash—a powdered igneous rock. So keep your eyes open and look for igneous rocks in your neighborhood. ■

WHAT DID WE LEARN?

- What is the difference between magma and lava?
- How are extrusive rocks formed?
- How are intrusive rocks formed?

TAKING IT FURTHER

- Which kind of igneous rocks have the largest crystals?
- Why is granite commonly used in buildings and monuments?
- Do all rocks sink in water?
- Why not?
- Where are you likely to find pumice?

Rocks & Minerals

IDENTIFYING IGNEOUS ROCKS

Once you have determined that a rock sample is an igneous rock, there are several things you can look at to decide exactly which kind of rock it is.

First, examine the crystal size. If the crystals are very small or nonexistent you know that it is an extrusive rock. If the crystals are large and easily visible then you know it is an intrusive rock. Some rocks have large and small crystals in the same sample. This is called porphyritic texture. Porphyritic rocks are intrusive rocks that began cooling slowly then shifted to an area that was cooler and cooled more quickly. Pumice, basalt, and obsidian are common extrusive rocks. Common intrusive rocks include granite and diorite.

Color is also helpful in determining what kind of rock it is. Rocks containing a high percentage of silica are light colored. Rocks with a low silica content are darker. Lighter rocks high in silica include pumice and rhyolite. Darker rocks include obsidian, basalt, and scoria. Granite is a combination of quartz, feldspar, and mica.

Depending on the exact combination of these minerals in a particular sample, granite can be very light or dark in color.

Some rocks have a high glass content making them very shiny. The best example of this is obsidian, which is often called glass rock or natural glass.

Finally, some igneous rocks formed from very bubbly lava. Gas bubbles were inside while they cooled; thus the rocks have a porous appearance. Porous rocks could include pumice and scoria.

Purpose: To test samples of igneous rocks

Materials: several samples of igneous rocks

Procedure:

1. Describe the color and the grain or crystal size for each rock.

2. Examine it for holes indicating that it had bubbles at one time.

3. Examine it with a magnifying glass and see if you can identify more than one kind of mineral in it.

4. Using a rocks and minerals guide, try to identify what each sample is.

SEDIMENTARY ROCKS

Layers of sediment

LESSON

11

How are sedimentary rocks formed?

Words to know:

strata

fragmental rocks

chemical rocks

Challenge words:

lithification

clast

conglomerate

breccia

matrix

BEGINNERS

Have you ever seen rocks with lots of lines in them? Then you have probably seen sedimentary rocks. Sedimentary rocks are made when little bits of rock, sand, dirt, or sea shells are washed away by moving water. When the water slows down, the bits of rock and other things settle to the bottom of the lake or ocean. As these little pieces pile up they can become stuck together, and minerals in the water act like glue. Once the water dries up, the pieces of dirt and sand dry and become rock.

The great Flood of Noah's day moved large amounts of dirt, sand, and rocks around. When the floodwaters dried up, they left behind most of the sedimentary rocks that we see today.

One common type of sedimentary rock is called sandstone. You can easily break off bits of sand from a sandstone rock. Limestone is another common sedimentary rock.

Not all sedimentary rocks were formed by the Flood. Some sedimentary rocks are man-made. Clay bricks are made from bits of clay mixed with water. Also, sidewalk chalk is made from bits of gypsum mixed with a special chemical and then dried. So, the next time you make pictures on the sidewalk, you can remember that you are using a man-made sedimentary rock.

- **How is a sedimentary rock made in nature?**

- **When were many of the sedimentary rocks formed?**

- **Name one common sedimentary rock.**

Have you ever seen the side of a mountain that looked like lots of flat layers of rock piled on top of each other? Maybe you saw this along the side of the highway where the rock had been blasted away to make room for the road. If so, then you have seen sedimentary rock.

Sedimentary comes from the Latin word *sedo*—meaning to settle down. Sedimentary rocks are formed as layers of sediment are bonded together by natural cement as they settle out of a water solution. This sediment can be tiny bits of rock, sand, dirt or seashells, along with chemicals or minerals that were dissolved in the water. Sedimentary rock usually forms in layers called strata (shown here). These layers are generally horizontal, but can become tilted as the ground shifts.

Sedimentary layers are called strata.

Sediment is mixed in water as the water moves over it. When the water slows down, the sediment settles to the bottom. As additional layers are deposited, the combined weight begins to press the layers more tightly together. In addition, minerals that are dissolved in the water work as a natural cement to glue the layers together. Eventually, these layers of sediment can harden and become sedimentary rock.

Most creation scientists believe that much of the sedimentary rocks on earth today were made as the sediment settled from the great waters of Noah's Flood. This would account for the large number of fossils found in the sedimentary rocks around the world.

Sedimentary rocks are grouped into two categories by how they are formed. Fragmental rocks are formed when fragments of other rocks are cemented together with pressure. A common fragmentary rock is sandstone. Sandstone is made as bits of quartz and grains of sand are "glued" together by silica, calcite, or iron oxide. Other common fragmental rocks include mudstone and shale, which are formed from fragments of silt and clay. Clay bricks are a man-made sedimentary rock.

Dolomite

The second type of sedimentary rock is chemical rock. Chemical rocks form when a chemical that has been dissolved in the water slowly precipitates out of the water or is left behind as the water evaporates. Chemical rocks do not form strata. One type of chemical rock is dolomite, shown here. Dolomite is formed from calcium and magnesium. Limestone is one of the most common chemical sedimentary rocks. It is

MAKING SEDIMENTARY ROCK

Purpose: To make your own sandstone

Materials: sand, cornstarch, water, saucepan, stove, paint

Procedure:

1. Combine 2 cups of sand, 1 cup of cornstarch, and 1 cup of water in an old saucepan.

2. Slowly heat this mixture over medium heat, stirring constantly until it is thick.

3. Remove it from the heat and allow it to cool. When it is cool enough to handle safely, mold it into a sculpture.

4. Allow the sculpture to harden. Then, if you desire, paint the sculpture.

Conclusion:

This is similar to how sandstone is formed. The pressure of your hands is like the pressure of the water and other layers on top of the sandstone. What "chemical" was used to cement the sand together? (Cornstarch) Natural sandstone is usually cemented by calcite or silica.

Wind and water wear away exposed sandstone. Look at this picture of sandstone arches from Arches National Park in Utah. This is a beautiful example of a sandstone formation resulting from erosion by wind and water.

MAKING A SEDIMENTARY LUNCH

You can make a sedimentary lunch by layering bread, peanut butter, and jelly to form a sedimentary treat! Lunchmeat and cheese would work, too.

formed when calcite precipitates from seawater. Many limestone deposits are filled with fossils of sea creatures. Limestone cliffs and caves can be found throughout the world.

Limestone is very important to man and has many uses. Lime is one of the key ingredients in cement. Also, real chalk is made from limestone. However, most of today's chalk, especially sidewalk chalk, is actually made from gypsum instead of limestone. Sidewalk chalk is another man-made sedimentary rock! ■

WHAT DID WE LEARN?

- How are sedimentary rocks formed?
- Were all sedimentary rocks formed during the Flood?

TAKING IT FURTHER

- Why are fossils found in sedimentary rocks?
- Sediment is simply any small piece of something that settles out of a liquid. What sediment might you find around your house or in nature?

LITHIFICATION

The process by which sediment is turned into sedimentary rock is called **lithification**. Lithification involves two things. First is the compression of the sediments. This generally occurs as more sediment is deposited. The weight of the sediment above compresses the sediment in the lower layers. This compression forces out air pockets and presses the sediments closely together.

The second part of lithification is the cementing of the sediments. This can involve a number of different chemicals, but the most common chemicals that glue sediments together are calcite and silica.

As we mentioned earlier, there are two kinds of sedimentary rocks, fragmental and chemical. Another name for fragmental rocks is clastic rocks. Geologists generally refer to the fragments that are cemented together as **clasts**. If the clasts are fairly large, 0.08 inches (0.2 cm) or larger, the rocks that are formed are called either conglomerate or breccia (BRECH-ee-uh).

Conglomerate rocks (shown at left) are formed when smooth rounded clasts are glued together. Conglomerate can contain any kind of clasts, but most of the stones in conglomerate are quartz. These

stones were rounded by erosion before they became part of the conglomerate rock. **Breccia** (shown above) is formed when jagged or angular clasts are cemented together. Again, these clasts can be composed of any kind of igneous, sedimentary, or metamorphic rock. The material that cements the clasts together is called the **matrix**. The matrix may be very smooth or very grainy depending on what it is composed of.

Purpose: To make your own conglomerate and breccia samples

Materials: two paper cups, plaster of Paris, smooth and jagged pebbles, spoon

Procedure:

1. In a paper cup combine ¼ cup plaster of Paris and ¼ cup smooth pebbles.

2. Add enough water to moisten the plaster. Then mix it together and press down on the mixture with a spoon to remove any air bubbles.

3. In a second paper cup combine ¼ cup plaster of Paris and ¼ cup jagged pebbles.

4. Again add enough water to moisten the plaster. Then mix it together and compress the mixture with a spoon.

5. Allow both cups to sit overnight.

6. When the mixture is dry, peel away the cups.

Conclusion: You now have a sample of conglomerate and a sample of breccia. Compare your samples with pictures of conglomerate and breccia above or in a rocks and minerals guide. How are they the same? How are they different?

FUN FACT

Clay is a man-made sedimentary rock. In the 1400s, a special type of orange clay called *pygg* was used to form clay pottery and dishes. Often people would store their money in a pygg container. Eventually, the type of container changed but the name remained and a pygg bank became what we today call a *piggy bank*.

FOSSILS

How do we know what dinosaurs looked like?

LESSON 12

How are fossils formed?

Words to know:

fossil

cast fossil

mold fossil

Challenge words:

coprolite

gastrolith

BEGINNERS

When you hear the word **fossil**, what do you think of? You may have thought of a dinosaur. But only a very, very small number of fossils are from dinosaurs or other large animals. Almost all fossils are fossils of sea creatures, mostly clams, snails, and other shellfish.

An animal can become a fossil only if it is covered with mud or sand very soon after it dies. If it is not covered quickly, it will decay and not become a fossil. It is believed by creation scientists that most animals that became fossils were covered with mud during the Genesis Flood. The floodwaters moved tons of mud and dirt around, and this mud covered millions of sea creatures that eventually became fossils.

If an animal dies and is quickly covered with mud or sand, the hard parts such as shells or bones can slowly be replaced by chemicals that are in the water that moves through the mud or sand. These chemicals harden into sedimentary rock and become fossils. This is why fossils are only found in sedimentary rocks.

• What kinds of animals are most fossils?

• Why don't most animals become fossils?

• What kind of rock contains fossils?

One of the most interesting aspects of sedimentary rock is that fossils are often found in them. **Fossils** are evidence of plants and animals from a previous time that has been preserved in the rock.

A fossil is formed when an animal or plant is quickly covered by mud, wet sand, ice, or tar. If it is not covered quickly, the organism will decay and disappear. After it is covered, minerals slowly replace the bones, scales, shells, and other parts of the animal that do not quickly decay. Eventually, all of the hard structures and sometimes some soft structures are replaced with minerals and become rock. A fossil is not an actual bone from a dinosaur or other creature; it is a rock in the exact shape of that bone.

Because fossils only form when a creature is covered shortly after it dies, fossils do not ordinarily form. An unusual event is required for a fossil to form. So why are fossils so common if they do not ordinarily form? The best explanation is that most fossils formed as a result of the worldwide Flood of Noah's time. Such a large flood would have suddenly covered millions of plants and animals with tons of mud and wet sand. This would result in an abundance of sedimentary rock formations filled with fossilized remains, which is exactly what we find in all parts of the world—even in Antarctica!

MAKING YOUR OWN FOSSILS

There are two different kinds of fossils that can be found in the rocks. One kind is called a cast fossil. A cast is a fossil that is just the imprint of the animal or plant that has been preserved in the dried mud. For example, if an animal stepped in wet sand or mud and left an imprint, and then the imprint was filled with sediment before it was washed away, a cast fossil of the animal's footprint could be made.

The second type of fossil is what we commonly think of as a fossil, and is called a mold fossil. Mold fossils are made when sedimentary rock slowly replaces the bone, shell, or other hard structure of the animal.

Purpose: To make your own fossils

Materials: shell of other object to "fossilize," petroleum jelly, modeling clay, Plaster of Paris, cup

Procedure:

1. Choose a shell or other object to "fossilize."

2. Put a thin coating of petroleum jelly on the outside of the shell.

3. Press the shell into a piece of modeling clay and remove the shell. You now have a cast fossil of the shell.

4. Pour about ¼ cup of Plaster of Paris powder into a cup and stir in enough water to make a smooth, but not runny, liquid.

5. Pour this liquid into the clay cast of the shell and allow the plaster to harden for several hours.

6. After the plaster is hard, gently remove the clay. You now have a mold fossil of the shell.

Cast

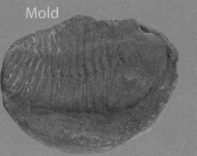

Mold

What can fossils tell us? They show us what kinds of plants and animals lived in the past. We see from fossils that most of the plants and animals in the past are very similar to those we see today. This is what we would expect to find since the Bible says that God created plants and animals to reproduce after their own kind. We also see that many kinds of plants and animals no longer exist—they have become extinct.

What we do not see from the fossils is one kind of creature slowly changing into another kind. Evolution teaches that some fish eventually, over a very long period of time, developed legs to use on land. But all fossils that have been found either have fins or legs. None has been found with something in between.

The most famous fossils are fossils of dinosaur bones. Although these creatures are interesting, they account for a very small portion of all the fossils. Ninety-five percent of all fossils are marine invertebrates—mostly shellfish; 4.75% of the fossils are algae and plant fossils; 0.2375% of all fossils are insects, and 0.0124% are fish. That leaves only 0.0001% of all fossils that are mammals, reptiles, or other large creatures. And of these, 95% consist of only one bone. There are very few examples of dinosaur fossils. On a line that is 10 feet long, 9½ feet of the line would represent the marine fossils and only 1/100th of an inch would represent the dinosaur fossils. The fossil record clearly indicates conditions consistent with a marine catastrophe such as a huge flood.

Human fossils are seldom found. There are many reasons for this. First, humans and land mammals tend to float when drowned and would not easily be covered by mud. Also, human bodies disintegrate very quickly so do not fossilize well. And finally, even if there had been 350 million people on the earth at the time of the Flood, and every one of them was preserved, there would be only one fossilized human for each 350 cubic miles (1,440 cubic km) of sedimentary rock. The chances of finding one would be very small. ■

WHAT DID WE LEARN?

- How does an animal become a fossil?
- What are the two different types of fossils?
- What types of creatures are most fossils?

TAKING IT FURTHER

- How many true transitional fossils, ones showing one kind of creature evolving into another kind, have been found?
- What does this indicate about the idea that land animals evolved from sea creatures?
- What are some things we can learn from fossils?
- What kinds of things cannot be learned from fossils?

TYPES OF FOSSILS

Fossilized footprints

Rock fossils include cast and mold fossils as you learned from the exercise you just completed. The vast majority of these fossils are bones, shells, and other hard parts of animals. But plants have left fossils behind as well. Other unusual fossils include footprints, called *trace fossils*. Many dinosaur and other animal footprint fossils have been uncovered in sedimentary rocks (see photo at top right). Another type of fossil is worm burrows. When animals are covered with large quantities of mud, many of them try to burrow out from under the heavy load. This sometimes results in fossilized burrows or tubes.

Petrified wood is also a type of fossil (shown below). Petrified wood is formed when a tree is encased in hot silica-rich water. The chemicals seep into the wood and eventually replace all of the organic material. Other items have become petrified besides wood. Animals and even some humans have become petrified when their bodies have ended up in a location

with hot silica-rich water. This form of fossilization does not take millions of years as some scientists would have you believe. Many tests have been done and petrification can happen in only a few years.

Other types of rock fossils are given special names. **Coprolites** are fossilized animal dung. This may sound disgusting to you, but scientists can learn about an animal's diet by examining coprolites from that animal. Gastroliths are another special kind of fossil. **Gastroliths** are groups of smooth stones that are found inside an animal's body. We know today that some birds swallow stones to aid in digesting their food. Evidently some dinosaurs did this as well, since piles of stones have been found inside some of the fossilized dinosaur remains.

Although we said earlier in the lesson that a fossil is evidence of plants and animals in the past that have been preserved in rock, most scientists actually recognize a broader definition of fossils as just evidence of plants and animals from the past. Although most fossils are rocks, some evidence of past plant and animal life comes in other forms. A different form of fossilization occurs when an animal or plant is completely covered by something that preserves the entire

creature. Many insects have been encased in amber, which is liquid tree sap. This sap eventually hardens and turns into a rock but the insect is preserved inside (see photo below). Although you may have heard that DNA can be extracted from the blood inside these trapped insects, this has not been accomplished. DNA lasts only a short time after death, and attempts to recover DNA from insects in amber have been unsuccessful.

Finally, some animals and even a few humans have been preserved in ice. It is very rare that an entire animal is frozen all at once, but a few mammoths and at least one person have been found encased in ice. Many millions of mammoth bones and parts of other animals have been found frozen. It is likely that these fossils were preserved during the Ice Age following Noah's Flood.

Petrified wood

Insect in amber

FOSSIL FUELS

A major energy source

LESSON 13

What are fossil fuels and where do they come from?

Words to know:

fossil fuels

Challenge words:

geologic column

BEGINNERS

Coal is an important type of sedimentary rock. It is burned for fuel in many power plants and has been used to heat homes and other buildings. While some plants buried during the Great Flood turned into fossils, many more plants turned into coal. Coal is made when plants are buried and then experience great heat and pressure. Because coal is made from plants that lived in the past it is called a **fossil fuel.**

Another fossil fuel is oil. Do you think of dinosaurs when you think of oil? Some people do. But oil has nothing to do with dinosaurs. Oil was produced when millions of tiny sea creatures were buried and then experienced high temperatures and pressure. Oil is usually found trapped in sedimentary rocks that contain fossils of sea creatures.

A third type of fossil fuel is called natural gas. Natural gas is usually found near oil deposits and many people believe that the gas was produced when the oil was formed. So coal, oil, and natural gas are all made from plants and tiny animals that lived in the past and are the main sources of energy for our cars and homes today.

- What are the three types of fossil fuels?
- What is coal made from?
- What is oil made from?
- What do we use fossil fuels for?

Have you ever heard the term *fossil fuels*? Did you picture a dinosaur or other creature and wonder what it had to with fuel? Fossil fuels refer to coal, oil, and natural gas. All of these fuels are believed to be the result of plants and animals that were buried in the past and, with time, heat, and pressure, changed into the forms of energy we use today.

Coal is considered by most scientists to be a sedimentary rock, although some geologists classify it as a metamorphic rock because it has been changed by heat and pressure. Either way, coal was formed from the remains of plants and thus contains a high amount of carbon that produces a large amount of energy when burned.

One quarter of the world's coal reserves are found within the United States.

Evolutionists believe that coal formed when decaying plants in swampy areas, about 300 million years ago, were slowly covered with sediment. The weight of the sediment eventually produced enough pressure to change the plants into coal. However, there are several problems with this theory. First, carbon-14 dating has shown some coal to be only a few thousand years old. Using carbon-14 dating, scientists have placed the age of some oil at only 4,200–4,900 years, which is much less than the millions of years given by evolutionists, and is about the date of Noah's Flood.

Additionally, large boulders have been found in coal deposits, indicating swift currents not stagnant swamps existed where the coal was formed. And finally, there are well-preserved delicate fern fossils in some coal beds, which would not be the case if these beds were formed from swamps over long periods of time. The evidence better supports the biblical view that prior to the Flood the climate was more tropical, encouraging larger plant growth than today, and that these plants were quickly buried by mud and other sediment during the Flood. These buried plants eventually changed into coal.

Contrary to what many people believe, it does not require millions of years to turn plants into coal. Coal has been formed in a laboratory in as little as eight months. All that is needed is high pressure and temperature. At the site of the Mount St. Helens volcanic eruption, plant debris that was buried in 1980 is already turning to peat, simply waiting for heat and pressure to turn into coal. So the large coal deposits we find today are easily explained by the Genesis Flood. (For more on coal formation, see www.answersingenesis.org/go/coal.)

Petroleum, or oil, is the liquid fuel formed from the remains of sea creatures (such as fish), plants, and algae. Oil is usually found in sedimentary rock containing marine fossils. Again, evolutionists say that oil formed slowly over millions of years. However, recent studies have shown that oil can only form in an area that traps gas and liquid in order to form the needed pressure to change the creatures into oil. Since no seal in rock is perfect, over time the liquid and gas will escape. The very existence of large oil fields, many of which have very high pressure, indicates that the fields can be only a few thousand years old, not millions of years old since the

The plant debris buried in the Mount St. Helens eruption is already turning to peat.

FOSSILIZED BONES

Purpose: To help us understand how fossils form as minerals replace bones or shells

Materials: two sponges, shallow dish, Epsom salt, food coloring

Procedure:

1. Cut two sponges into bone or shell shapes and set one piece aside to use for later comparison.

2. Place the second piece in a shallow dish or pan.

3. Pour one cup of hot water into a separate bowl and stir in as much Epsom salt as will dissolve in the hot water.

4. Add a few drops of food coloring if desired.

5. Pour the salt water over the sponge in the dish and set the dish in a location where it will not be disturbed for several days.

6. After several days compare the original sponge with the "fossilized" sponge.

Questions:

• How does the original sponge feel compared to the "fossilized" sponge?

• How does the original sponge look compared to the "fossilized" sponge?

Conclusion:

The "fossilized" sponge is larger because the holes were filled while the sponge was wet and expanded (this is a side effect of sponges and does not happen with actual fossils). Also, you should be able to see salt crystals in the holes in the sponge. This is how chemicals that harden into rock replace the bone or shell, by filling in the holes and then hardening. The "fossilized" sponge may also look white and powdery compared to the original one. Actual fossils do not necessarily have the same color as the original bone or shell.

gas would have escaped and the pressure reduced long ago. In addition, oil has been formed in a laboratory in a matter of minutes or hours. All that is needed is the right amount of temperature and pressure.

Natural gas is the gas form of fossil fuels. It is often found along with oil and is believed to be a by-product of the oil formation process. The very existence of natural gas under pressure indicates relatively recent formation, only a few thousand years ago. The next time you hear the term fossil fuel, you can picture plants and sea creatures, instead of dinosaurs, turning into coal, oil, and natural gas. ■

WHAT DID WE LEARN?

• What is the definition of a fossil fuel?

• What three forms of fossil fuels do we commonly use?

TAKING IT FURTHER

• What evidence supports rapid and recent coal formation instead of slow formation millions of years ago?

• Why is finding natural gas when drilling into the ground a good indicator that oil is nearby?

• Why is the existence of natural gas an indication that oil was formed only a few thousand years ago?

GEOLOGIC COLUMN

Just as there is confusion about whether dinosaurs were the animals that turned into oil, there is often a lot of confusion about when and how fossils were made and when the fossilized plants and animals actually lived. In the 1600s and 1700s it was discovered that fossils of particular plants and animals were usually found together in a particular area. For example, one set of rocks may contain fossils of particular kinds of fish, shellfish, and other aquatic creatures, while another set of rocks may contain fossils of giraffes, saber-toothed tigers, and land plants. These different collections of fossils have been grouped into 12 different sets.

At that time, most scientists looked at the fossils found in different layers of rock and concluded that they were formed during Noah's Flood and that the different layers of fossils represented the different

ecosystems that were destroyed during the Flood (i.e., the order of burial). This is still the view held by most creation scientists today. The layer of rocks containing primarily sea-bottom-dwelling creatures would have been buried first and formed the lowest levels of fossils. Those containing land-dwelling animals would have formed later in the Flood and would be found above the layers of aquatic fossils.

However, in the 1800s the idea that the earth is very old became popular. That is when scientists began to believe that the different layers of rock represented different time periods and that the different fossils found in each layer represent the animals that were dominant on the earth at that time. This is used to support the idea of evolution, supposedly showing that sea creatures slowly evolved into land-dwelling creatures.

Evolutionists have taken the 12 groups of fossils and stacked them one on top of another to represent a geologic time line with the fossils in the lowest layers representing animals that lived up to 500 million years ago. It should be noted that nowhere in the world are all 12 layers found in the order given in this geologic column. And there are some instances in which layers are found in the "wrong" order.

Evolutionists claim that this column demonstrates the evolution of species from simple water-dwelling creatures to complex land-dwelling creatures. However, there are no fossils that demonstrate this. First, there are no fossils that are part way between one kind of animal and another. There are no fossils of creatures that have something in between fins and legs. All fossils show animals that have either fully developed fins or fully developed legs, but nothing in between. Second, the fossils of many supposedly simple creatures show that these creatures are really quite complex. Also, many of the fossils show that even the oldest creatures are often very similar to animals that live today. This is strong evidence for fossils being formed by the Flood and not for millions of years of evolution.

Now complete the "What Would You Expect?" worksheet to see how different ecosystems could result in different animals in different fossil layers.

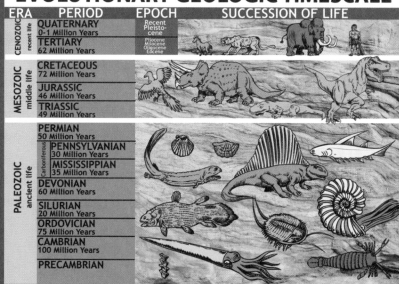

METAMORPHIC ROCKS

Let's make a change

LESSON 14

How are metamorphic rocks formed?

Words to know:

foliated

BEGINNERS

So far we have learned about two different kinds of rocks: igneous rocks are made when melted rock cools and hardens; sedimentary rocks are made when bits of dirt, sand, and rock are glued together and form a new rock. Now we are going to learn about a third kind of rock. This kind of rock is called metamorphic rock. That's a big word, but don't let the name scare you; *metamorphic* just means changed, so you could call them changed rocks.

Metamorphic rocks are rocks that have been changed from one kind into another kind. When igneous or sedimentary rocks end up inside the earth, they sometimes get placed under a great deal of pressure. And because the inside of the earth is very hot, they also experience a great deal of heat. If these conditions last for a long time, the rocks eventually change into different kinds of rocks. This is why we call them changed or metamorphic rocks.

These changed rocks are usually very hard. Marble is one kind of metamorphic rock that is very hard. It is often used to make sculptures and buildings. It is also very beautiful and can be polished.

- **What does the word *metamorphic* mean?**

- **What does a rock have to experience to become a changed rock?**

- **Name one kind of metamorphic rock.**

W̲e have learned that igneous rock is formed when magma cools, and sedimentary rock is formed when small bits of sediment are pressed and cemented together. The third category of rock is metamorphic rock. The word *metamorphic* comes from the Greek word meaning "to change form." Metamorphic rock is igneous or sedimentary rock that has been changed into a different form. These rocks were changed due to the heat and pressure inside the earth's crust over a period of time.

Gneiss, a metamorphic rock

Metamorphic rocks are divided into **foliated** and nonfoliated rocks. *Foliated* comes from a word meaning "with leaves." Obviously these rocks do not have leaves like trees, but they do have flattened crystals that line up in parallel layers, so they break easily into thin broad sheets that somewhat resemble leaves. A common example of a foliated rock is slate. Slate is formed when shale, a sedimentary rock, has experienced pressure and heat over time to become a very hard rock. Another foliated rock is gneiss (pronounced like *nice*). The bands in the above photo of gneiss are clearly visible. Gneiss can be formed from several different sedimentary and igneous rocks including granite, diorite, and hornblende.

Nonfoliated metamorphic rocks do not have lines or layers. Two common nonfoliated metamorphic rocks are quartzite and marble. Marble is limestone that has been changed. Pure marble is white, but many marble deposits contain impurities that result in the common swirled appearance often associated with marble. Marble is hard

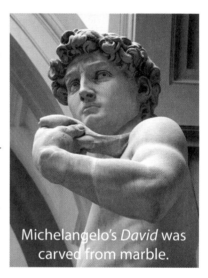

Michelangelo's *David* was carved from marble.

MORPHING ICE

Follow the directions and answer the questions for the "Morphing Ice" worksheet.

MAKING MARBLE

Purpose: To demonstrate why marble often has a swirled appearance

Materials: two or three pieces of taffy, waxed paper

Procedure:

1. Unwrap two or three pieces of different colored soft candy such as taffy and place them on top of each other.

2. Wrap the candy in a piece of waxed paper and press the candy together for at least a minute.

3. Unwrap the candy and look at it.

Conclusion:

The striped appearance should resemble the swirled appearance of marble. Marble is formed when limestone is pressed and heated for a long time. The swirled appearance occurs because other types of rock may be intermixed with the limestone formation.

and holds a polish so it is often used for sculptures, monuments, floors, and buildings. Quartzite is changed sandstone. Heat and pressure rearrange the quartz crystals resulting in a very hard stone. Quartzite is the same color as the sandstone from which it came and can vary from tan, to brown, to red. ■

WHAT DID WE LEARN?

- What are the three ingredients needed to change igneous or sedimentary rock into metamorphic rock?

- Why is marble often swirled instead of pure white?

TAKING IT FURTHER

- Why is metamorphic rock often used for sculptures and monuments?

- Why is metamorphic rock hard and durable?

TYPES OF METAMORPHIC ROCKS

Complete the "Metamorphic Match" worksheet.

ARTIFICIAL ISLANDS

Natural islands develop in many ways. One of the most spectacular ways is when a volcano erupts under water and the lava builds up until it breaks the surface of the water and a new island is born. But why would someone want to build an artificial island? Usually islands are built to provide someone with more land to use. But this is not the only reason.

One of the earliest artificial islands was built in Puget Sound near Seattle, Washington. But it wasn't made to make more land. It was the result of opening up a channel for shipping at the mouth of the Duwamish River. The builders had to do something with all the dirt they dug up, so they made an island. This project was started in 1900 and took nine years to complete. Using a process called dredging, they brought up soil from the bottom of the channel. Most of the soil, 24 million cubic yards (18 million cubic meters) of it, was used to form what is now called Harbor Island. Upon completion, the island was nearly 350 acres (140 hectares) and at that time it was the largest man-made island in the world.

Only one person lived on the soggy island for the first couple of years. He lived there with his dog, an angora goat, and about 300 chickens. He didn't own the island, but for a time no one cared. Then, in 1911, he had to leave when a shipyard was built on the island. In 1918, during World War I, two of the largest wooden steamers in the world were built at this shipyard.

The island wasn't without its problems. Because it was built on top of the river delta and the land is seismically unstable, it moved a fair amount during earthquakes. In 1949 parts of the island rose 16 inches (40 cm) while other parts fell 12 inches (30 cm). In the earthquake of 1965, two of the piers on the island moved one foot (30 cm) closer to Seattle. In 2001, when seismologist Bob Norris was on the island during an earthquake, he described muddy water erupting from the ground. This made him think that a water main had burst. He described what looked like geysers, shooting water into the air about 3 feet (1 m) high. He later found out that the muddy water was a result of the liquefaction of subsurface soil during the earthquake. Liquefaction is when loose soil becomes fluid-like during an earthquake.

Although Harbor Island was built because engineers needed a place to put tons of extra soil, several other man-made islands have been built for the purpose of providing more land. One of the more notable islands is off the coast of Japan, near the city of Osaka. This island (pictured on the previous page) was built for the purpose of making land for an airport. Japan is a rather crowded country, and airports take up a large amount of valuable land. So an island was built specifically for the new airport. The island is connected to the mainland by a 2.33 mile (3.75 km) long bridge. The bridge was built with two levels: there is a highway on the top level and a railway on the lower level. The airport only has one runway, but it can handle about 438 takeoffs and landings a day. The airport has 33 passenger gates.

The airport opened on September 4, 1994, and has only one big problem. This 1.95 square mile (5 square km) island is sinking. The designers planned for this, however, and the airport was built with hydraulic jacks under it that can raise and lower the terminal as needed. Parts of the island are sinking faster than other parts, and some people feel that the hydraulic jacks are just barely able to keep up. But an airport spokesman said that even though the jacks are raised regularly, there is no danger and the sinking is within expected limits.

The problems with this man-made island have not deterred Japan from building more artificial islands. A second island was started in August 2000 to house another airport. This new island has a circumference of about 5 miles (8 km). It is only about 0.6 miles (1 km) offshore near the city of Tokoname, which is located near the geographical center of Japan in the Ise Bay. The airport opened in 2005.

Japan is not the only country working on artificial islands around the world. The country of Abu Dhabi is building an island called "Lulu Island," a 1,050-acre (61-hectare) island for a Disneyland-style amusement park.

However, the biggest artificial island project underway is in the Persian Gulf, off the coast of Dubai in the United Arab Emirates. The Palm Islands are three islands that will be large enough to see from the moon! Each of the islands is being built in the shape of a palm tree and consists of a trunk and a crown with fronds. They will each be surrounded by a crescent island that acts as a breakwater. The islands will support luxury hotels, residential villas, water homes, shoreline apartments, marinas, water theme parks, restaurants, shopping malls, sports facilities, health spas, cinemas, and various diving sites.

Palm Island Resort as photographed from the International Space Station

To build each island, the builders will use about 100 million cubic yards (76 million cubic meters) of dirt and rock. In 2006 the first residents moved in. They hope to have the first two islands fully opened by the end of 2009. The largest of the Palm Islands will be 8.7 miles (14 km) long and 5.3 miles (8.5 km) wide and have a land area of 31 square miles (80 square km).

As technology improves, artificial islands may become more common in the future. So watch the news for new places to visit.

Minerals

Animal, vegetable, or mineral?

LESSON 15

What are minerals and how do we use them?

Words to know:

mineral

native mineral

Beginners

Now that you have learned about different kinds of rocks, you might want to know what rocks are made of. They are made of minerals. But what is a mineral? In order for something to be considered a **mineral**, it has to be a solid; this means it cannot be a liquid or a gas at regular temperatures. It also has to occur naturally; it cannot be made by man. And it has to be made of something that was never alive; that means it is not made from a plant or animal. Also, if you could look at the way the tiny pieces of the mineral are put together, you would see that they form crystals. The crystals may be big enough to see, or they may be so small that you would need a special microscope to see them.

There are lots of minerals around your house, and you use minerals every-day. Salt is a mineral that you probably eat every day. You will find other minerals in your food as well, including calcium, zinc, and iron. Some minerals that you don't eat include gold, silver, and copper.

Many of the things you consider rocks are actually minerals. Some minerals that look like rocks are quartz, mica, and feldspar. You can find these minerals by themselves. But if they have been combined together into one rock, that rock is called granite. You can learn more about rocks and minerals by studying pictures and descriptions in a rock and mineral guide book.

• How do you know if something is a mineral or not?

• Name at least three minerals.

I n lesson 9 we learned that rocks are made of one or more minerals or organic materials. But what is a mineral? In order for a substance to be considered a **mineral**, it must meet all five of the following requirements.

1. Naturally occurring—not put together by man

2. Inorganic—is not and has never been alive. All plants and animals have carbon in their cells, so anything that is carbon-based is considered organic.

3. Definite chemical structure—always has elements in the same proportion. For example, quartz is always two parts oxygen to one part silicon.

4. Atoms are arranged in a regular pattern—for example, a crystalline structure

5. Solid—at normal temperatures

Minerals that have only one type of atom are called **native minerals**. They are pure elements. Native minerals include most of the metals such as gold, silver, and copper. Also, even though diamonds are made from carbon, geologists make an exception and classify them as a native mineral.

Most minerals, however, are made of more than one type of element. For example, table salt contains both sodium and chlorine in equal amounts. Minerals that are not comprised of a pure element are called *compounds*. Most minerals are compounds.

Substances that contain more than one element in varying proportions are called *mixtures* and are not considered minerals. For example, granite is a rock that contains feldspar, quartz, and mica. However, two samples of granite will likely have different ratios of the three minerals. One may have more feldspar than quartz; another sample may have more quartz than feldspar. Therefore, granite is a rock but is not a mineral. Most rocks are mixtures of minerals.

Minerals are very important to our lives. We make many items out of minerals such as jewelry made from gold and silver and money made from nickel and zinc. Common minerals you may find around your house include salt, alum, quartz, fluoride, gold, silver, and copper. Also, our bodies need minerals to keep them healthy. Look at a box of cereal and see all of the vitamins and minerals that are added to help keep you healthy. ■

Mica

Amethyst Quartz

MINERAL SCAVENGER HUNT

Complete the "Mineral Scavenger Hunt" worksheet.

WHAT DID WE LEARN?

- What five requirements must a substance meet in order to be classified as a mineral?
- What is a native mineral?
- What is a compound?

TAKING IT FURTHER

- Are there any minerals that are mixtures?
- What is the difference between a rock and a mineral?
- Is coal a mineral?
- Are all minerals considered rocks?
- Are all rocks considered minerals?
- Where are you likely to find minerals?

MANCALA

Rocks and minerals have so many uses we could not list them all in this book, but one of my favorite ways to use rocks and minerals is to play the game Mancala. Mancala is one of the oldest games and originated in ancient Egypt or the Middle East.

Purpose: To use rocks to play Mancala

Materials: egg carton, small pebbles or stones, coin

Procedure:

1. Cut the top off of an egg carton, and then cut the top in half.

2. Tape one half to each end of the carton bottom to form a bin at each end. These are called the mancalas.

3. Place four small pebbles or stones in each of the cups in the egg carton.

The game is now set up for two players. The mancala on your right is yours and the mancala on your left is your opponent's mancala.

Game Instructions:

Flip a coin to decide which player goes first. The first player selects a cup on his side of the board and takes all of the stones out. He then drops one stone in the cup to the right of the one he took the stones out of. He continues dropping one stone into each cup in a counter-clockwise direction. If he comes to the end of his side of the board, he drops a stone in his mancala and continues on around to his opponent's side of the board until he uses all of his stones. Never drop a stone in your opponent's mancala. If you drop your final stone into your mancala, you get another turn. If you have the right number of stones so that you drop your final stone into an empty cup on your side of the board, you get to move

that stone and any stones that are in the cup on the opposite side of the board into your mancala. This is called a capture. You cannot make a capture from your opponent's side of the board. Continue playing until one player no longer has any stones on his side of the board. The player with remaining stones gets to place all remaining stones in his mancala. The player with the most stones in his mancala at the end of the game wins.

This is a fun game of strategy. It is simple to learn but difficult to master. There are also many variations on the rules. Once you understand the basic rules, you may want to try to play with different rules. You can look online for different variations of this game.

IDENTIFYING MINERALS

Is it salt or sugar?

How can we identify different minerals?

Words to know:

luster

cleavage

fracture

BEGINNERS

When you pick up a rock from the ground, did you ever wonder what kind of rock it was? It is not always easy to identify a particular rock or mineral. However, you can do a few tests to help you figure out what it might be. One of the easiest things you can do is look at the color of the rock. This will give you an idea of what type of rock it might be. You can also look at how shiny the rock is. Is it sparkly, shiny, or dull? This quality is called **luster**, and it helps you decide what kind of rock or mineral you have.

Another thing you can look for is crystals. Look closely at your sample and see if there are any crystals. If there are, decide if they are big or small and what shape they are. These all help you identify your sample. Once you make all of these observations, you can use a rocks and minerals guide to help you decide what kind of rock or mineral you have.

If you want to know more details about how to identify rocks and minerals, you can read the rest of this lesson and try doing some of the tests that are described here.

- What are three things you can look for to help you identify a rock or mineral?

S ome minerals are easily identifiable by simple observation, while others are easily confused. With practice, you will be able to identify rock and mineral samples more easily. But even with practice, some samples can be difficult or tricky to identify. Geologists have devised a series of tests to help determine what mineral a sample contains.

- Color: This is a starting point in determining what mineral your sample contains. Some minerals have distinctive colors, especially if the samples are pure. However, color is not adequate to identify most minerals. Impurities can change the color. Quartz, for example, can be green, pink, blue, violet, or smoky. Also, oxidation, or rust, can change the outward color or appearance of a sample. Besides, many minerals have the same color as other minerals.

- Streak: A more accurate way to determine the color of a sample is to perform a streak test. Rub the sample across a piece of unglazed porcelain or ceramic tile and examine the color of the powder left behind. Even if a sample's color has been changed by impurities, its streak will remain pure. Note: minerals that are harder than the tile will not leave a streak.

- Luster: This is a description of the quality and intensity of light reflected from the surface. For example, a sample of pure copper will have a metallic/shiny luster. Other samples could have a luster classified as glassy, pearly, adamantine (sparkling like a diamond), fibrous, silky, greasy, or dull.

- Crystal shape: Minerals have a regular shape. Some minerals have hexagon, cubic, needle, or rosette-shaped crystals. Others have crystals that are too small to see with the eye. A magnifying glass is useful to help determine the crystal shape.

FUN FACT

Your body is full of minerals. It contains:
- Enough calcium to make 340 sticks of chalk
- Enough phosphorous and sulfur to make 250 boxes of matches
- Enough sodium and chlorine for 40 teaspoons of table salt
- The amount of fluoride found in 30 tubes of toothpaste
- Enough iron for 6 paper clips
- The amount of potassium found in 500 bananas
- Enough magnesium for 182 anti-acid tablets

Here are some minerals and the foods that contain them:
- Calcium—found in dairy products
- Phosphorus—found in milk, cheese, and dried beans
- Sodium—found in salt, milk, tomatoes, celery, and meat
- Fluoride—found in most drinking water. Don't eat your toothpaste—it can be hazardous to you.
- Iron—found in meat, dried beans, breads, and cereals
- Potassium—found in bananas and other fruits, soybeans, mushrooms, and breads
- Magnesium—found in whole grains, potatoes, and many fruits

By eating a wide variety of foods, you will get the vitamins and minerals necessary to keep you healthy.

Just as with igneous rocks, the temperature at which the mineral formed greatly affects the size of the crystals. Those formed at higher temperatures and cooled slowly have larger crystals than those that formed quickly at lower temperatures. Some minerals, which formed very quickly, may have no crystals at all.

- Hardness: A scratch test is used to determine how hard a mineral is. Something that is hard will scratch the surface of something that is softer. Using substances with known hardness will help you determine the hardness of your sample. In 1812 the German mineralogist Friedrich Mohs created the Mohs scale, which characterizes the scratch resistance of various minerals. For example, talc is one of the softest minerals and is assigned a hardness of 1 on the Mohs scale. Diamonds are the hardest known mineral and are assigned a hardness of 10. Quartz has a hardness of 7, and calcite has a hardness of 3. Samples of these known minerals can help determine the hardness of your sample by using one material to try to scratch another material.

- Cleavage: This is a test of how well a sample breaks in straight lines. Using eye protection is a must when performing this test. Using a hammer, break the sample

MINERAL IDENTIFICATION

Use masking tape to label each mineral sample with a number. Using a copy of the "Mineral Identification" worksheet, record your observations as you perform each of the following tests.

1. **Color**—Record the color and any other observations for each sample.

2. **Streak**—Firmly press the sample against an unglazed tile and make a streak. Record the color of the powder (if any).

3. **Luster**—Record the luster of the sample (glassy, sparkly, shiny, oily, metallic, etc.).

4. **Crystal shape**—Use a magnifying glass to observe the crystal structure. Record the shape and size.

5. **Hardness**—Try to scratch the sample with a fingernail and a penny. Test if the sample will scratch the side of an old drinking glass. On the Mohs scale, a fingernail has a hardness of 2.5, a penny is 3.5 and glass is 5.5. Record the relative hardness of the sample. (Less than 2.5, between 3.5 and 5.5 or greater than 5.5.)

6. **Cleavage**—Place the sample in an old pillowcase or wrap it in a towel. **Be sure to wear eye protection such as goggles.** Use a hammer to break the sample. Observe how it cracks or breaks.

7. Using these observations and a rocks and minerals guide, try to identify each sample. Information for some common minerals is included below:

Mineral	Color	Streak	Luster	Crystal	Hardness	Cleavage
Talc	White	White	Dull	None	1	None—thin flakes
Gypsum	White to gray	White	Pearly	Flat	2	Perfect in 1 direction
Mica	Clear to gray	Clear	Sparkly	Flat	2.5	Thin sheets
Calcite	Clear, white, pink	White	Shiny	Triangular	3	Perfect 6-sided crystals
Fluorite	White, green, pink	White	Sparkly	Cube or 8-sided	4	Perfect 8-sided
Feldspar	Pink	White	Shiny	4- or 6-sided, flat	6	Varies with type
Pyrite	Brassy to gold	Green/black	Shiny	Cubic	6–6.5	Perfect in 3 directions
Quartz	White, pink	White	Glassy	Hexagon	7	Fractures
Topaz	Colorless to green	White	Glassy	Rectangular	8	Perfect in 2 directions
Diamond	Clear	None	Sparkly	8-sided	10	Perfect in several directions

into two pieces. Examine the broken edges to see if the sample broke in straight lines. Samples that break in flat sheets are said to have perfect cleavage. These samples break this way because the crystals are tightly bonded in one direction but weakly bonded in another direction. An example of a mineral with perfect cleavage is mica, which breaks into flat sheets, usually with just a fingernail. Other samples may have good, fair, poor, or no cleavage. Some minerals do not have cleavage but break along smooth curves. These minerals are said to have fracture. An example of a mineral with good fracture is obsidian, which has been used to make arrowheads and other tools.

Scientists often must perform other tests as well in order to determine the composition of a sample. However, these other tests may be difficult or dangerous to do at home. They include:

- Flame test—The color of the flame of a burning sample can help identify it.

- Acid test—Some minerals react with acids to produce a bubbling/foaming reaction.

- Magnetism—Some minerals are magnetic.

- Radioactivity—Some minerals are radioactive and can be tested with a Geiger counter.

- Glow test—Some minerals have fluorescence (they glow in ultraviolet light).

- Refraction—Some minerals bend light that shines through them. ■

WHAT DID WE LEARN?

- What are some common tests used to identify minerals?

- Why is color alone not a sufficient test?

TAKING IT FURTHER

- Is crystal size a good test for identifying a mineral? Why or why not?

- What is the difference between cleavage and fracture?

- Why do some tests need to be done in a laboratory?

- How can you tell a sample of sugar from a sample of salt?

ROCKS AND MINERALS

Recall that in lesson 15 we talked about three different categories for rocks and minerals. Specimens that contain only one kind of atom are called native elements. Specimens that contain several elements combined together to form a new substance are called compounds. Finally, if several compounds are combined together in varying proportions, the substance is called a mixture. Minerals are never mixtures; they are always native elements or compounds. Most rocks are mixtures of minerals.

Use a rocks and minerals guide to help you complete the "Is it a Rock or a Mineral?" worksheet.

VALUABLE MINERALS

How much for an ounce of gold?

Which minerals are valuable and why?

BEGINNERS

In lesson 15 you learned that you use minerals everyday. Salt and calcium are both minerals. But some minerals are more expensive than others. If a mineral is hard to get, it is said to be scarce, and if it is scarce and it is important for some reason, it becomes a valuable mineral. One of the most valuable minerals is gold. It is hard to find large amounts of gold, so gold is considered scarce. And gold is important for many reasons. It is considered very beautiful and is often used for jewelry and art, it is soft and therefore easy to make into nearly any shape, and it does not rust. Therefore, gold is considered a valuable mineral.

Silver is also a valuable mineral, but it is not as expensive as gold because more silver than gold has been found in the earth's crust. Silver is used for jewelry, and can be used for making electronic circuits. It is also a very important ingredient in film for photographs. Silver and gold have been used for making coins for hundreds of years because they are both valuable minerals.

Another valuable mineral is copper. Copper is easier to find than silver or gold, so it is less expensive. Copper is used for many purposes including electrical wiring for houses and other buildings and for copper pipes and copper pots.

Finally, diamond is a very valuable mineral. Diamond is the hardest known mineral. Diamonds form beautiful crystals that sparkle in the light. They are used for jewelry if they are clear, and they are often used for drill bits if they are not. All of these valuable minerals were created by God for us to use and enjoy.

- Name four valuable minerals.

- What is the hardest mineral?

- What are some uses for valuable minerals?

As far back as we have records, and even among civilizations without written records, we see that man has recognized the beauty and usefulness of many minerals. The Bible shows that the earliest civilizations valued gold, bronze, and iron. It says in Genesis 4:22, "And as for Zillah, she also bore Tubal-Cain, an instructor of every craftsman in bronze and iron." Tubal-Cain was the great grandson of Cain and had the knowledge to work with bronze and iron. And in Genesis 2:11–12 it says that one of the rivers flowing through the Garden of Eden also flowed through the land of Havilah, "where there is gold." Also, paintings and archeological finds reveal many uses of gold, silver, iron, and other valuable minerals in even the oldest post-Flood civilizations. God created minerals, rocks, and gems in their various forms for man to use and enjoy.

Many of the more valuable minerals are the native minerals. Recall that native minerals are the minerals that are pure elements—they have only one kind of atom. Valuable minerals are usually expensive because they are very useful or beautiful and are limited in quantity. Generally, the more abundant an element is, the less expensive it is.

Men working a sluice box to find gold in the Yukon territories, circa 1900

One of the most desired minerals is gold. Gold is valued for its beauty and usefulness. Because gold is one of the heaviest minerals, it has often been mined from riverbeds by panning or sluicing. In this type of mining, the miner scoops up dirt from the bottom of the river, then allows water to wash away the lighter materials, leaving the heavier gold behind. In the early gold rush days in California and Colorado, panning for gold was the easiest way to find nuggets. However, the gold in the riverbeds was soon exhausted and drilling into the mountains revealed the largest finds of gold.

Over the centuries gold has had many uses. Gold has been used for money, jewelry, and in dentistry. It doesn't tarnish or rust and it conducts electricity so it is also useful for electrical contacts in semiconductors.

Silver is more common than gold, so it is less expensive. Yet silver is still considered a precious metal. It is often used for jewelry and tableware. It is the best metal for conducting electricity, so it is used in electrical circuits. Silver is also very important in the processing of photographic film. Also, silver and gold have been used to make coins for hundreds of years. However, today most coins are made from zinc and other less expensive materials.

Another important mineral is copper. Copper is mostly mined in the form of copper sulfide ore. These ores are abundant in New Mexico and Arizona. Copper is useful for many purposes as well. Because copper conducts electricity nearly as well

CHOCOLATE MINING

Mining is almost always required to remove valuable minerals from the earth's crust. Gold and silver nuggets are seldom found just sitting by themselves waiting to be discovered. Instead, miners must removed tons of ore—rock that contains the desired mineral—along with other elements, and then process the ore to remove the mineral.

Purpose: To appreciate the work required to mine for gold, silver, or diamonds

Materials: chocolate chip cookie, toothpick

Procedure:

1. Carefully remove each chocolate chip from the cookie by using only a toothpick.

2. After the chips are removed, describe the appearance of the cookie.

3. Enjoy the chocolate chips you "mined," and then be sure to clean up the area (by eating the crumbs.)

Questions:

- How difficult was it to "mine" the chips from the cookie?

- Does what's left over look anything like the original cookie?

Conclusion: Mining is a difficult and messy process. It can be devastating to the ecology of an area if miners are not careful. In the past, miners came and took what they wanted, leaving behind a destroyed area. Today, miners are more careful to restore an area after mining.

as silver, but does not tarnish as quickly and is less expensive, it is used for electrical wiring in most buildings. Copper pipes are used for plumbing and copper is used for making pots and pans. Copper is used for jewelry and for sculptures, as well.

Most metals, such as gold, silver, and copper, are found in the earth's crust in the form of oxides or sulfides. Oxides are minerals that have combined with oxygen. Sulfides are minerals that have combined with sulfur. Ores containing these oxides and sulfides are mined and then processed to remove the native minerals.

A final native mineral that is very valuable is diamond. By definition, minerals do not contain carbon, which is the basis of organic/living material. This is why coal is not considered a mineral. However, geologists make an exception for diamonds. Diamonds are made from pure carbon that has been crystallized. Diamond is the hardest known mineral. It is given an absolute hardness of 10 on the Mohs scale compared to glass with a hardness of 5.5 and fingernails with a hardness of 2.5.

Diamonds have perfect cleavage, allowing the light to sparkle through them. Uncut diamonds have a greasy luster, but cut diamonds have a very brilliant sparkly luster called *adamantine*. Diamonds are mostly used for jewelry. Their value is determined by their size, color, purity, and cut. Diamonds that are not useful as gems are used in other capacities. Because of their hardness they are often used on the tips of drills and saws that are used to cut other hard materials. All of these valuable minerals were created for our pleasure and use by our wonderful Creator. ■

FUN FACT

Valuable metals have been used for many interesting purposes. For example, the Statue of Liberty is made from sheets of copper laid over an iron framework. The dome on the Colorado state capitol building is covered in very thin sheets of 24-karat gold, called gold leaf. And although salt is very inexpensive today, during the Roman Empire salt was so valuable it was used as a form of money.

WHAT DID WE LEARN?

- What are some valuable minerals?
- What is a native mineral?
- What are some important uses for gold?
- What are some important uses for silver?

TAKING IT FURTHER

- Why is diamond considered an exception among minerals?
- Diamonds and coal are both made from carbon. What makes them different?

NATIVE MINERALS

There are 19 native minerals—minerals that occur as pure elements. These native minerals are divided into three groups: the metals, semimetals, and nonmetals. The metals include platinum, iridium, osmium, iron, zinc, tin, gold, silver, copper, mercury, lead, and chromium. You have probably heard of most of these native minerals because metals are used in many applications in our daily lives.

The semimetals are materials that have some metal characteristics and some nonmetal characteristics. For example, they may conduct a small amount of electricity, but are not considered good conductors. The native minerals that are semimetals include bismuth, antimony, arsenic, tellurium, and selenium. You have probably not heard of most of these elements; however, selenium is a very

important native mineral because of its semiconducting properties. It is used in photovoltaic cells, which are solar cells that convert solar energy into electricity. Selenium can also be used in medical procedures as a tracer element. This means it can be injected into the body and traced to see where it goes. This allows doctors to follow the flow of blood throughout a patient's body.

The third category of native minerals is the nonmetals sulfur and carbon. These two native minerals have many uses. We have already mentioned the many uses of diamonds, the most valuable form of carbon. Sulfur is one of the most useful elements for nearly every industrial purpose. Usually sulfur is combined with other elements for industrial purposes. One of the most common uses of

sulfur is in sulfuric acid. Sulfuric acid is the most produced chemical in the United States. The biggest use of sulfuric acid is in the making of fertilizers. It is also used to make car batteries, paints, plastics, and many other manufactured items. In fact, sulfuric acid is so important to manufacturing that some economists use a country's use of sulfuric acid as an indicator of how well that country's economy is doing. Sulfur is much more abundant than diamonds or gold and is often found in locations near volcanoes.

Chose a native mineral that you are not familiar with and research it. Find out what that mineral is used for and why it is important. Share your findings with your parent, teacher, or class.

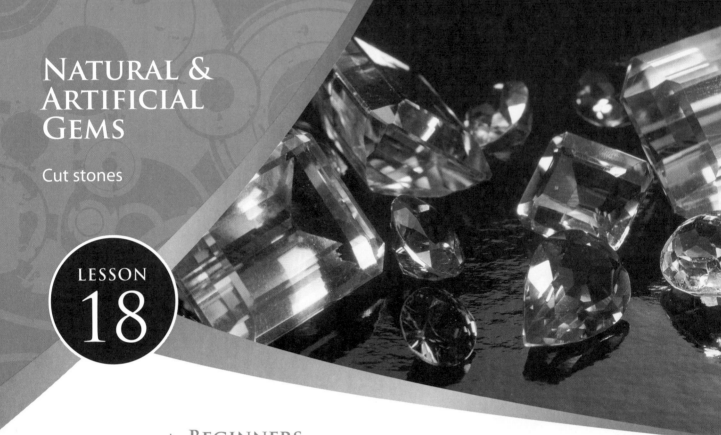

Natural & Artificial Gems

Cut stones

LESSON 18

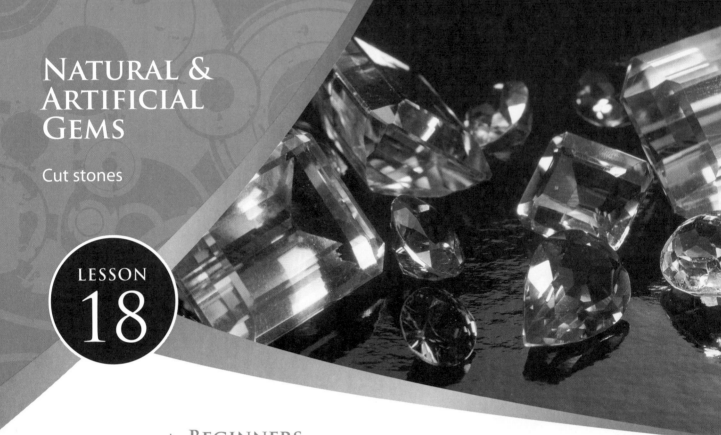

What are gems and how are they made?

Words to know:

gem

Beginners

Have you ever seen a diamond ring sparkling in the light? How about a ruby or an emerald? Stones such as these, which can be polished or cut to reflect light, are called **gems**. Other popular gems include sapphire, topaz, and amethyst. Gems were important to people even in Bible times. The high priest in the Bible wore a special breastplate that contained 12 different precious stones (Exodus 28:15–21).

Most gems are fairly expensive because they are somewhat scarce. To allow people to wear beautiful gems at a lower cost, scientists have figured out how to make many artificial, or man-made gems. Sometimes the artificial gems are made from the same material that the natural gem is made from. The material is melted at very high temperatures and then allowed to slowly cool and turn into crystals. Other times the artificial gems are made from different materials from the naturally occurring gems, but look very much the same.

Although artificial or man-made gems may look similar to the natural ones, they are not as strong as the natural ones. God's design is always better than man's design.

- What is a gem?

- What are three common gems?

- How are man-made gems different from natural gems?

Just like gold and silver, gemstones have had significant uses since the beginning of civilization. One of the most important references to gems in the Bible is in Exodus 28:15–21, when God commanded Moses to place special stones on the breastplate of the high priest. There were four rows with three stones in each row. Each stone was to represent one of the twelve tribes of Israel. These gems were important for the Old Testament worship of God.

Another important reference to gems in the Bible is in Revelation 21:9–21. This passage describes what the New Jerusalem will look like. It says the foundation of the New Jerusalem will be made from jasper, sapphire, emeralds, and other precious gems.

Gems are minerals that are popular because of their beautiful colors or designs, and their ability to be polished or reflect light in a brilliant way. Most gems have perfect cleavage and can be cut in ways that reflect the light.

Popular gemstones include ruby, diamond, emerald, sapphire, topaz, and amethyst. Today, gems are used mostly as jewels and for decorations.

Naturally occurring gems are relatively scarce or limited in quantity. Therefore, they are fairly expensive. Usually, the more scarce a gem is, the more expensive it is. So, because of people's desire to possess gems, and their relative scarcity, scientists have worked to create synthetic or man-made gems.

Artificial gems

Early copies or substitutes for gems can be found as far back in history as ancient Egypt. Samples of artificial gems made from glass or ceramic have been found in many ancient Egyptian sites. Today, colored glass is less likely to be used but not completely unheard of. More recently, scientists have been successful in growing crystals from the same minerals that compose the naturally occurring gems.

In 1954, scientists produced the first man-

BREASTPLATE WORKSHEET

Read Exodus 28:15–21. The high priests during the time of Israel's temple worship were very important. The high priest was responsible for offering sacrifices for the sins of the nation of Israel. Today, we no longer need a high priest to offer sacrifices because Jesus was the ultimate sacrifice for our sins and Jesus has become our high priest. However, it is still important to understand the pattern of Old Testament worship.

Color the gems on the "Breastplate" worksheet. Suggested colors for each stone are listed below the picture.

made diamonds from carbon atoms. The temperatures required were greater than 4,800°F (2,650°C), and the pressure was greater than 1.5 million pounds per square inch (100,000 kg/cm²). Although these copies were very close to naturally occurring diamonds, they were very small and useful only for industrial applications. More recent attempts to make man-made diamonds have resulted in larger diamonds, but ones that are not pure in color. Most substitute diamonds that are used as gemstones today are made from cubic zirconium, not carbon.

Synthetic rubies are made by melting the minerals in rubies at high temperatures and then allowing them to cool and crystallize. Many other synthetic gems are made this way as well. It is a fairly fast process, taking only months for crystals to form. However, these synthetic stones are less expensive than naturally occurring stones.

Often, synthetic gems look very similar to their natural counterparts. However, differences are easily seen under a microscope or magnifying glass. Synthetic gems are often "too perfect." Naturally occurring gems have slight imperfections. Also, synthetic gems are not as durable as the natural ones. No matter how good man's efforts are, they are a weak imitation of God's original design. ■

WHAT DID WE LEARN?

- What is a gem?
- How is a gem different from a native mineral?
- How are artificial rubies made?

TAKING IT FURTHER

- What can you guess about the temperatures at which synthetic rubies are formed?
- Why would rubies be formed at high temperatures?
- What are some disadvantages of synthetic gems?
- Why are natural gems worth more money than artificial gems?

BEAUTIFUL GEMS

Since gems are something valued for their beauty, it is helpful to actually look at gems to see how beautiful they are. Using a gems book or the Internet, look at pictures of many different gems. If you have access to a color printer or copier, make copies of the pictures and compile your own book of gems. Looking at gems on paper is good, but looking at gems in person is even better. If you have a chance, visit a jewelry store and view some of the many beautiful gems that they have available there. Many museums have rock and mineral collections where you can view many of the rocks and minerals that we have studied.

UNIT **3**

MOUNTAINS &
MOVEMENT

PLATE TECTONICS

Slip sliding away

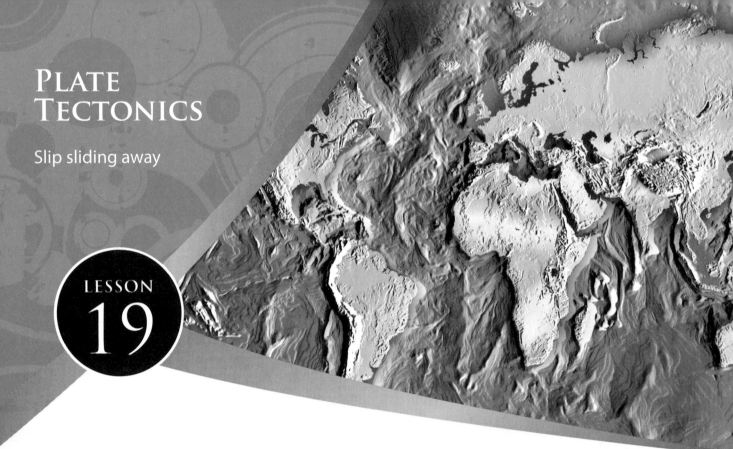

LESSON

19

What is plate tectonics and how has it affected the earth?

Words to know:

plate tectonics

Rodinia

Challenge words:

subduction zone

subduction

rifting

strike-slip faulting

BEGINNERS

If you look at a map of the world you will see that there are areas of land and areas of water. The large pieces of land are called continents and the large areas of water are called oceans. Today there are seven continents and four oceans, but most scientists believe that at one time there was only one large continent. This continent has been given the name Rodinia.

Many creation scientists believe that when God caused the Genesis Flood, the crust of the earth cracked to allow the water that was trapped below ground to shoot up. This was where most of the water came from for the Flood. These cracks in the earth's crust allowed the land to break up into pieces that we call plates and move apart to form the continents that we have today.

- What are large areas of land called?

- How many continents do scientists think existed before the Flood?

- What is that continent called?

Until the 1960s, most scientists believed that the earth's crust was one solid piece of rock that was completely stationary. But the idea that the earth's crust is actually several large pieces floating on the mantle has become the more accepted theory in the last 40–50 years. This idea is called **plate tectonics**.

This idea was first proposed in 1859 by creation scientist Antonio Snider, who suggested that crustal plates moved horizontally during the Flood of Noah's time. Then, in 1912 German geologist Alfred Wegener suggested that all of the continents we see today were originally one landmass. But because he could not explain what would cause the plates to move, his theory was largely ignored. Later, Arthur Holmes suggested that the earth's crust is actually several large plates floating on liquid magma, and that slow movement of these plates, called continental drift, is what caused the single landmass to break up into the different landmasses we see today.

Creation scientists agree that there was originally one landmass and that the crust is now made up of plates that float on the magma. This original landmass has been named **Rodinia**. But most creationists reject the idea that slow continental drift is adequate to explain the movement of such gigantic landmasses. Instead, the evidence shows that this shifting happened in a relatively short period around the time of the Genesis Flood. This view has been called Catastrophic Plate Tectonics.

The Bible says in Genesis 1:9, "Let the waters under the heavens be gathered together into one place, and let the dry land appear." So, it appears that originally there was one landmass and one ocean. Genesis 7:11 says, "all the fountains of the great deep were broken up." The Hebrew word for "broken up" is *baqa*, which means cleaving or faulting. This could very well be describing the breaking of the earth's crust into the plates that we see today. There may have been another supercontinent called Pangaea that assembled midway through the Flood. Creation scientists think Rodinia probably

PANGAEA PUZZLE

Purpose: To see how the continents may have appeared before they broke apart into today's landmasses

Materials: tracing paper, map of the world, tape

Procedure:

1. Place a piece of tracing paper over a map of the world and trace the continents.

2. Cut out each of the continents and try to piece them together to form one landmass.

3. Tape the pieces together to form "Pangaea."

FUN FACT Where did all that water go after the Flood? If the entire earth's surface were leveled by smoothing out the topography of not only the land surface but also the rock surface on the ocean floor, the waters of the ocean would cover the earth's surface to a depth of 1.7 miles (2.7 km). We need to remember that about 70% of the earth's surface is covered by water. Quite clearly, then, the waters of Noah's Flood are in today's ocean basins.

came apart early in the Flood, with its pieces slamming back into each other later in the Flood, forming a mostly submerged Pangaea. Pangaea then came apart and emerged near the end of the Flood, with its pieces forming today's continents.

It is believed that there are 13 tectonic plates: 6 major plates, each about the size of a continent, and 7 minor plates that are significantly smaller. It is also believed that many of the fold and fault mountain ranges were formed when the continental plates moved as a result of the Flood. Today, the tectonic plates move very slowly and can cause earthquakes and volcanic activity, resulting in faults and rifts in the earth. ■

WHAT DID WE LEARN?

- What is plate tectonics?
- How many plates do scientists think there are?

TAKING IT FURTHER

- What are some things that are believed to have happened in the past because of the movement of the tectonic plates?
- What are some things that happen today because of the movement of the tectonic plates?

PLATE MOVEMENTS

Continental drift is the name given to the movement of the tectonic plates of the earth's crust today. These plates move in three main ways. Plates can move toward each other, away from each other, or slide against each other. Each of these movements can cause earthquakes or volcanic eruptions and can have other effects on the earth's surface as well.

The collision of two plates together creates a subduction zone, and subduction occurs when one of the plates is pushed down

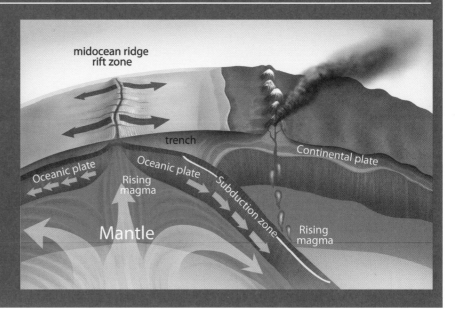

Mountains & Movement

below the other plate. The lower plate is pushed down into the earth's mantle and some of it may melt. Subduction occurs most frequently when an oceanic plate is pushed below a continental plate. Subduction is believed to be the source of much of the volcanic activity along the Pacific rim "ring of fire."

Rifting occurs when two plates move away from each other. This is occurring along the Mid-Atlantic Ridge below the Atlantic Ocean. When rifting occurs, a space opens between the plates allowing magma to push up between the plates and spread out in either direction. This forms new land, usually on the ocean floor. This process is often called sea-floor spreading.

The third way that plates move is horizontally against each other. This horizontal movement is called **strike-slip faulting**. Faulting can create large amounts of sediment as the plates rub against each other. And occasionally the plates get stuck against each other and pressure builds up. When the pressure is high enough, rocks break and the plates lurch forward causing an earthquake.

San Andreas fault zone, Carrizo Plains, central California

Purpose: To demonstrate each of these plate movements

Materials: waxed paper, peanut butter or frosting, graham crackers

Procedure:

1. Spread a thick layer of creamy peanut butter or frosting on a piece of waxed paper. This represents the magma of the earth's mantle.

2. Place two graham crackers on top of the peanut butter to represent two tectonic plates.

3. Slide the crackers together and push one of them under the other. This represents subduction. Watch how the "magma" moves as the "plates" move.

4. Next, smooth out the peanut butter and set two crackers next to each other.

5. Move the crackers away from each other and watch as a space develops between the plates.

6. Push up from below the waxed paper and watch the peanut butter squeeze up between the plates. This movement represents rifting.

7. Finally, smooth the peanut butter out again and place two crackers next to each other.

8. With the edges pressed together, push one cracker away from you and pull the other cracker toward you. This represents strike-slip faulting. Watch for crumbs that are generated and look at how the peanut butter is moved around.

Conclusion: These exercises should give you an idea of what happens as the plates move. Remember that these plates today generally move very slowly, much more slowly than they would have moved during the Flood.

MOUNTAINS

Don't make a mountain
out of a mole hill

LESSON

20

What is a mountain?

Words to know:

elevation

actual height

BEGINNERS

Do you know what a mountain is? A mountain is an area of land that is taller than the land around it. It usually has steep sides going up to the top of the mountain. Some mountains are relatively short, while others are very tall. The tallest mountain on earth is Mount Everest.

Sometimes you may find a mountain by itself, but usually mountains are found in groups that form a sort of chain. A group of mountains is called a mountain range. Some of the most famous mountain ranges in America include the Cascade Range in Oregon and Washington, the Sierra Nevada in California, the Rocky Mountains in Idaho, Wyoming, Colorado, and New Mexico, and the Appalachian Mountains that run from Maine to Georgia.

- **What is a mountain?**

- **What is the tallest mountain in the world?**

- **Name one famous mountain range.**

You have probably been told, "Don't make a mountain out of a mole hill." This means don't make a problem bigger than it really is. But how can you tell if something is really a mountain or a just a hill? A mountain is an area of land that naturally rises higher than the surrounding land. It usually has steep sides rising to a summit. Mountains are taller or higher than hills in the same general area. The designation of *mountain* or *hill* is often dependent on the area in which the rise occurs. For example, a 500-foot (150-meter) rise in Wyoming would be called a hill, but a 400-foot (120-meter) ridge in New York is called the Watchung Mountains.

When describing a mountain, two different terms are often used. First, the **elevation** of a mountain is the height of the summit above sea level. For example, Mount Everest (shown here) has an elevation of 29,028 feet (8,848 m) and is said to be the highest mountain in the world. The second measurement for a mountain is its **actual height**. This is the difference between the

Mount Everest

elevation of the summit and the elevation of the base of the mountain. Because Mount Everest has such a high base, its actual height is only about 12,000 feet (3,650 m). On the other hand, Mauna Kea in Hawaii, has an elevation of 14,000 feet (4,260 m) but an actual height of 33,000 feet (10,000 m). How can its actual height be higher than its elevation? The base of Mauna Kea is 19,000 feet (5,740 m) below sea level!

A series of mountains in a given area is called a mountain range. And a group of mountain ranges is called a mountain system. The highest mountain system is the Himalya-Karakoram system, between India and China. More than 95 of the 109 mountain peaks in this system are over 24,000 feet (7,300 m) in elevation, including Mount Everest. The longest or most extensive mountain system is the Mid-Atlantic Ridge, which extends for 10,000 miles (16,000 km) under the Atlantic Ocean. It

FAMOUS MOUNTAINS

Complete the "Famous Mountains" worksheet.

FUN FACT

"PIKES PEAK OR BUST" was a famous slogan for pioneers heading west. Pikes Peak is one of the highest mountain peaks in Colorado, with an elevation of 14,110 feet (4,300 m) above sea level. It is located near Colorado Springs and is one of the first peaks people see as they head west into Colorado. It was first climbed in 1819 and was named for Zebulon Pike, who was the first white explorer to see it up close.

The summit of Pikes Peak was also the location from which Katherine Bates wrote the song, "America the Beautiful."

Every Fourth of July, there is a famous car race on the road up the side of Pikes Peak.

goes almost from pole to pole. To see it you have to be a deep sea diver because it is found on the floor of the Atlantic Ocean.

Some of the most famous mountain ranges in America include the Cascade Range in Oregon and Washington, the Sierra Nevada in California, the Rocky Mountains in Idaho, Wyoming, Colorado and New Mexico, and the Appalachian Mountains that run from Maine to Georgia. ■

WHAT DID WE LEARN?

- What is a mountain?
- What is a mountain range?
- What is the difference between actual height and elevation of a mountain?

TAKING IT FURTHER

- Where are the mountains with the highest elevations located?
- Is a 700 foot rise a mountain or a hill?

MOUNTAIN RANGES

The world today has many mountain ranges. These mountains play many important roles. Mountains have unique habitats for animals. They provide timber for us to use. Mountains also affect the weather in many areas. So it is important to know where the major mountain ranges are around the world.

Obtain a copy of a world map. Using an atlas or topographical map of the world, draw and label the following mountain ranges on your copy of the world map. Save this map for future lessons.

The Rocky Mountains

Major Mountain Ranges of the World

Alps	Caucasus Mountains
Ural Mountains	Himalaya Mountains
Great Dividing Range	Atlas Mountains
Andes Mountains	Sierra Nevada Mountains
Rocky Mountains	Appalachian Mountains

TYPES OF MOUNTAINS

How did they form?

How are the different types of mountains formed?

Words to know:

depositional mountain

erosional mountain

fold mountain

fault

Challenge words:

basin

dome

monocline

anticline

syncline

BEGINNERS

It can be fun to hike up a mountain or to ski down a mountain slope, but have you ever wondered where that mountain came from? The Bible indicates that God created the earth with some mountains, but scientists also think that many of the mountains that we see today were formed as a result of the Genesis Flood.

New mountains can be formed three different ways. First, some mountains have been made when rocks, sand, ash, lava, or other materials are moved from one place to another and piled up to form a mountain. This happens when a volcano erupts shooting out ash, rocks, and lava. Mountains can also be formed when water carries material from one place to another. Many of the mountains and sand dunes we see today were probably formed when the floodwaters carried material from one area to another.

A second way that new mountains can be made is when water, ice, or wind wears down an area and removes rock and other material, leaving behind a mountain of harder rock. These mountains usually have very steep sides and often have flat tops. The Flood is probably responsible for many of these kinds of mountains as well since the waters would have been able to wear down much of the land as they rushed over it.

Finally, mountains can be pushed up. Remember when we talked about how one big continent broke apart into pieces called plates to form the continents that we have today? Well, as the earth's crust moves, different plates push against each other. When one plate gets pushed on from two different sides, the land in the middle can get pushed up to form new mountains.

Many scientists believe that the mountains we see today were formed over millions of years, but the Bible indicates that the earth is not that old. Many of the mountains could have been formed as a result of the Flood of Noah's day just thousands of years ago.

- Describe three ways that new mountains can be made.

- What is the likely cause of many of the mountains we see today?

Where did mountains come from? Did God create the mountains the way they are today or have they changed over time? Not all scientists agree on how the mountains were formed. Genesis 7:19–20 says that the floodwaters covered the high mountains to a depth of 15 cubits (about 20 feet). So we know that God created the earth with some mountains. However, there is evidence that many of the mountains we see today formed as a result of the Flood and its aftermath.

Mountains are classified according to how scientists believe they were formed. Most mountains are classified as either depositional, erosional, or fold and fault mountains. **Depositional mountains** are ones that form from accumulated rocks,

Volcanic depositional mountain

volcanic lava and ash, sand, or other material. Volcanic mountains are the most likely to be observed as they are being formed. Erupting volcanoes can deposit lava, ash and rocks to form new mountains in a very short period of time. One of the most well-known examples of a volcano forming a mountain occurred in a farmer's field in Mexico. In 1943, this volcano suddenly appeared and deposited over 1,400 feet (425 m) of material in only one year's time. The picture to the left is Diamond Head, an extinct volcano on Oahu, Hawaii.

Other depositional mountains are formed when wind and water deposit lighter materials. For example, sand dunes are hills and mountains of sand that have been deposited by wind and water. The Flood could have easily carried tons of sand and debris and deposited them to form many of the sand dunes we see today. Finally, some of the mountains were formed as glaciers dragged large amounts of debris, depositing it in an area as the ice melted.

The second way that mountains form is through erosion. **Erosional mountains**

Sand dunes are a type of depositional mountain.

Erosional mountain

The largest mountain in our solar system is on Mars. Olympus Mons rises 78,000 feet (24 km) above the surrounding plain. Its base is more than 300 miles (500 km) in diameter.

are also called residual mountains. These are mountains that remain after the surrounding material has eroded away. Erosional mountains, like the ones in this picture, are usually flat on top and have steep sides. Most creation scientists believe that erosional mountains are a direct result of the Flood. The floodwaters laid down hundreds and even thousands of feet of sediment that formed into sedimentary rock. As the waters of the Flood receded, much of this rock was washed away. What remained hardened into the residual mountains that we see today.

Although there are many examples of depositional and erosional mountains, it is believed that most mountain ranges were formed by folding and faulting. The picture below demonstrates fold and fault mountains. Many scientists believe that when two tectonic plates, or sections of the earth's crust, push against each other, pressure is applied to the rocks. Eventually the rocks will either break or snap, resulting in an earthquake, or they will bend (called folding) or slip (called faulting). When the rocks bend and push up they form **fold mountains**. When they slip along a **fault** or crack in the earth's surface, and one section pushes up higher than another, fault mountains are formed.

Fold mountain

Although these are the commonly accepted classifications for mountains, there is considerable disagreement and room for much more research in this area. This is one area that creation scientists, those who accept the Word of God as true, can do more investigation and gain better understanding of God's creation. ■

PAPER FOLD MOUNTAINS

Purpose: To demonstrate how fold mountains form

Materials: newspaper or paper towels

Procedure:

1. Lay a few sheets of newspaper or paper towels on top of one another.

2. Slightly moisten the paper by sprinkling a small amount of water on the papers.

3. Place your hands on opposite edges of the papers, and then slowly push your hands toward each other. What happens?

Conclusion:

The papers should push up in the middle, forming fold mountains. This is similar to how many scientists believe that many mountain ranges were formed. They believe that when a tectonic plate is pushed on from two sides, the land is pushed up in the middle, forming mountains.

FOLD TYPES

As you just learned, most of the mountains we see today are either fold or fault mountains. We will discuss faults more in the next lesson. For now we will take a look at the forces that produce the different fold mountains that exist around the world. The type of folding that has occurred in fold mountain formation may not be obvious from the surface of the mountain; however, erosion, mining, or roadwork can expose the inside of a mountain, and the folding of the layers of the mountain become apparent.

There are five basic types of folding that can occur. If a downward force, such as gravity, overcomes other surrounding forces an area can sink resulting in a basin. This would appear to be a rounded depression in the earth, thus forming mountains around it. If a force is directly upward from inside the earth, a dome of rock can form. This would result in a rounded hill or smooth looking mountain.

If forces push up on one side of a rock formation and down on the other side, the rocks will rise up on one side and be compressed on the other. This forms what is called a monocline. If forces are applied from opposite sides of the rock formation and the rocks bend instead of break, they can either bend upward or downward. If the rocks bend upward the formation is called an anticline. If the rocks bend downward the formation is called a syncline.

It is believed that much of the folding of sedimentary rock occurred during or shortly after the Flood while the rock layers were still soft. You can experiment with how forces could move soft rock by using a moist sponge. Apply forces in different directions and see how the sponge moves. See if you can form a basin, dome, monocline, anticline, and syncline by applying forces in different places on the sponge.

Monocline

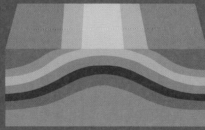

Anticline

Syncline

EARTHQUAKES

Shake, rattle, and roll

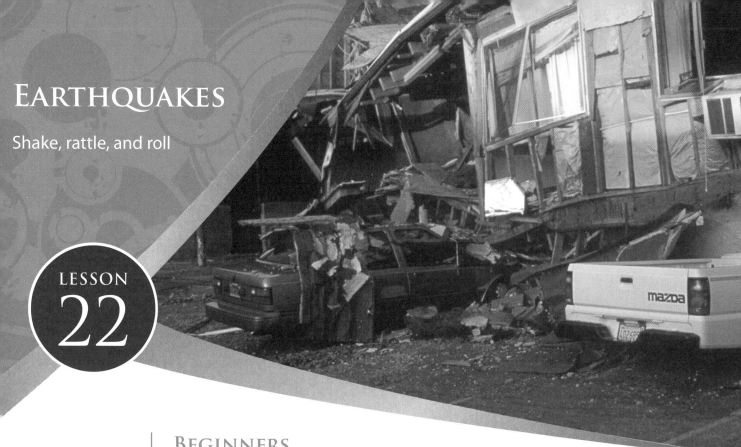

LESSON 22

. **What are earthquakes and how are they caused?**

Words to know:

earthquake

aftershock

focus

epicenter

tsunami

Challenge words:

footwall

hanging wall

normal fault

reverse fault

thrust fault

strike-slip fault

BEGINNERS

Have you ever experienced an earthquake? Probably not, but earthquakes happen every day. An **earthquake** is when the earth's crust suddenly moves. This movement is caused when two plates of the earth's crust push against each other until one of the plates slips. This happens several times a day, but most of the time the earthquake is too small for people to feel the movement. Strong earthquakes happen a few times each year.

A strong earthquake may not cause any damage if it occurs in a part of the world where there are not very many people. However, if the earthquake occurs in an area where there are lots of people, it can cause a great deal of destruction and even death.

A strong earthquake may be followed by several smaller earthquakes called **aftershocks**. Aftershocks can be felt for days or even weeks after the first earthquake. An earthquake can also trigger huge waves called **tsunamis**. These giant waves can crash into land that is near or land that is very far away from where the earthquake happened.

- How often do earthquakes happen?

- What is an aftershock?

- What is a tsunami?

Have you ever felt the ground move under your feet, seen the light fixtures swinging from the ceiling or heard dishes rattle in the cupboard without someone touching them? Probably not, unless you have experienced an earthquake. An earthquake is the rapid movement of the earth's crust. Elastic strain builds up in the rocks deep in the earth's crust as tectonic plates move against each other. This movement can be horizontal or vertical. When the strain becomes too great, the rocks break apart and rebound off of one another. This movement results in what we call an earthquake.

Earthquakes happen frequently, several times each day. However, most earthquakes are too weak for a person to detect. A few times a year, an earthquake occurs that is strong enough to feel, and occasionally strong earthquakes occur that can cause severe damage and even loss of life. Often, severe earthquakes are followed by many smaller quakes called aftershocks. Aftershocks may occur for several weeks after the original earthquake.

The center of activity for an earthquake is called the focus. The area on the surface of the earth above the focus is called the epicenter. The amount of damage or destruction caused by an earthquake depends on the location of the epicenter and the magnitude or strength of the quake. Earthquakes in uninhabited areas cause little damage. However, earthquakes in densely populated areas can cause widespread destruction and death. Even though the ocean is uninhabited, earthquakes that originate under the ocean can be the most deadly. These quakes can trigger huge waves called tsunamis. Tsunamis can be only two or three feet (0.5–1 m) high in the open ocean, but they grow much higher as they approach land. They can travel at speeds up to 500 miles per hour (224 meters per second) and cause extensive damage. Land-based earthquakes near the ocean can generate tsunamis as well. On December 26, 2004, an undersea earthquake in the Indian Ocean caused a tsunami that devastated the shores of Indonesia, Sri Lanka, South India, Thailand and other countries with waves up to 100 feet (30 m) high and killed more than 283,000 people.

Earthquakes move out in waves from the epicenter. These waves move like ripples in a pond when a rock is dropped into the water. Earthquake waves travel up to 16,000 mph (7,150 m/s) through rock and more slowly through soft sand and mud. There are three types of earthquake waves. P waves, or primary waves, are the fastest waves. They move through the ground like sound waves. S waves, or secondary waves, move more slowly. S waves distort as they pass through rock. The final type is called L waves, or long waves. L waves travel on the surface of the earth and often cause most of the damage.

Earthquakes most often occur along boundaries of tectonic plates. Faults are

FUN FACT

Nearly 90% of all earthquakes occur along the Circum-Pacific and Alpine-Himalayan volcano belts. The Circum-Pacific belt is roughly a circle around the Pacific Ocean and is called the "Ring of Fire." The other 10% of earthquakes can occur anywhere else in the world.

often found along these boundaries as well. A fault is a crack in the rock where the earth has moved. At one time, scientists thought these faults caused earthquakes. Today, we know that earthquakes cause the faults. One of the most famous faults is the San Andreas Fault, which runs from San Francisco, California south into Mexico. It is 700 miles (1,125 km) long and is located where the Pacific and American plates meet.

EARTHQUAKE-PROOF BUILDINGS

One of the major causes of death during an earthquake is the collapse of buildings. In America, in areas where earthquakes are likely to happen, buildings are often designed to withstand the movement of the earth. They are specially reinforced and some are even built on shock absorbers. However, in third world countries, many buildings are built with inferior designs and poor materials, and they easily collapse.

Purpose: To demonstrate the advantages of different building designs

Materials: building blocks

Procedure:

1. Build a corner of a building using building blocks arranged as in the first picture.

2. Gently shake the table on which the blocks are placed.

3. Increase the intensity of the "earthquake" until some of the blocks fall over.

4. Repeat this process for each of the building designs and note what happens.

5. Now, build a building of your own design and test its strength.

Questions:

- Which design was the strongest?

- Which design was the weakest?

- How did your design compare to the others?

- What might architects do to help make buildings stronger?

- What shape of building is more likely to withstand an earthquake?

In God's original "very good" creation, earthquakes probably didn't exist. God cursed the creation because of Adam's sin (Genesis 3, Romans 8), and as a result we now experience natural disasters, such as earthquakes and hurricanes. Below is a list of some of the deadliest and most destructive earthquakes in recent history:

- November 1, 1775: Lisbon, Portugal—60,000 died

  Damage occurred all the way down to North Africa. Most deaths were due to flooding caused by tsunamis.

- October 28, 1891: Mino-Owari, Japan—7,000 died

- April 18, 1906: San Francisco, California—5,000 died

  Water pipes broke from the earthquake, preventing firefighters from putting out a fire that burned for several days.

- September 1, 1926: Yokohama, Japan—200,000 died

  Most deaths were caused by fires that could not be put out.

- July 28, 1976: Tangshan, China—240,000 died

  The quake registered 8.2 on the Richter scale and was felt 500 miles (800 km) away.

- September 19, 1985: Mexico City, Mexico—4,000 died

  Most deaths were due to poor construction of buildings that collapsed on the people.

- December 7, 1988: Armenia—55,000 died

  500,000 people were left homeless. The quake registered 6.8 on the Richter scale, followed four minutes later by a quake of 5.8 magnitude.

- May 21, 2003: Algiers, Algeria—3,000 died

  A quake of 6.5 magnitude brought down many buildings on the people of Algeria.

- December 26, 2004: Indian Ocean off the coast of Sumatra—283,000 died

WHAT DID WE LEARN?

- What is believed to be the cause of earthquakes?
- What is an aftershock?
- What name is given to the area on the earth's surface above where an earthquake originates?
- What is a fault?

TAKING IT FURTHER

- How does the type of material affect the speed of the earthquake waves?
- How does this change in speed help scientists "see" under the earth's crust?
- Why are earthquakes in the middle of the ocean so dangerous?

FAULTS

Faults often occur because of earthquakes. Stress among the rocks causes a break in the rocks and a sudden shift causes the rocks to move. This movement can leave a crack in the earth's surface. It is also believed that faulting has caused the formation of many of the mountain ranges around the world.

There are three basic kinds of faults that can occur. If the break is at an angle from top to bottom then the rocks generally move vertically with respect to each other. If the break is vertical, then the rocks tend to move horizontally.

If you look at the normal fault below, the right side (the side below the fault) is called the **footwall** and the left side (the side above the fault) is called the **hanging wall**. When forces are applied, the footwall and hanging wall move with respect to each other.

If the hanging wall moves down with respect to the footwall, this movement is called a **normal fault**. If the hanging wall moves upward with respect to the footwall, it is called a **reverse fault** or a **thrust fault**. Reverse faults are nearly vertical while thrust faults are horizontal. If the crack is vertical and the rocks move horizontally with respect to each other, this is called a **strike-slip fault**.

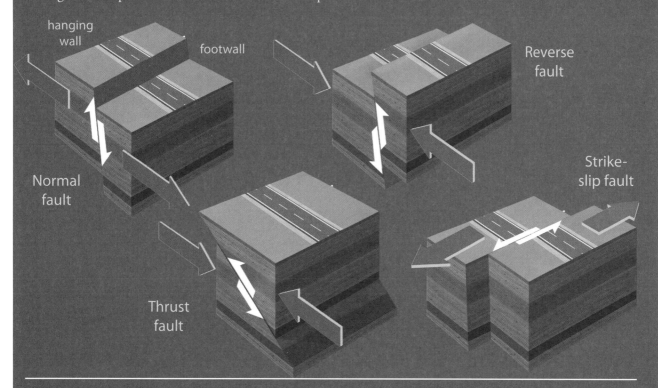

Purpose: To demonstrate each of these kinds of faults

Materials: three colors of clay, knife

Procedure:

1. Make three identical layers of clay about 1 inch thick from each of three different colors of clay.

2. Make three clay "sandwiches" with one color on top, a different color in the middle, and the third color on the bottom. These layers represent different layers of sedimentary rock.

3. Cut the first block of clay at an angle from top to bottom as shown in the diagram and slide the hanging wall down to represent a normal fault.

4. Cut the second block the same way, but slide the hanging wall up to represent a reverse fault.

5. Finally, cut the third block vertically and slide the pieces horizontally to represent a strike-slip fault.

DETECTING & PREDICTING EARTHQUAKES

Predicting the "Big One"

How can we measure and predict earthquakes?

Words to know:

seismograph

BEGINNERS

Because earthquakes can be very dangerous, scientists want to know when and where they happen. They use a special instrument called a **seismograph** to help show them where earthquakes are happening. There are thousand of seismographs around the world, so scientists can see where earthquakes are happening anywhere.

A seismograph has a cylinder or drum covered with paper and a special pen that writes on the paper. The drum can move with the earth, but the pen cannot so the pen makes marks showing how much the earth has moved in that location. This allows scientists to see earthquakes as they are happening around the world.

Scientists collect earthquake information and hope someday to be able to predict when and where earthquakes will occur. Right now, only God knows when an earthquake is going to happen. This doesn't mean that people can't do anything about earthquakes, though. People have learned to build buildings that are much stronger and can withstand the shaking that occurs during an earthquake. Stronger buildings are safer and help to save people's lives during an earthquake.

- What instrument is used to detect earthquakes?

- How can people make buildings safer during earthquakes?

- Can people accurately predict when and where an earthquake will happen?

Predicting when and where an earthquake will strike is a very difficult task. Scientists are still not able to predict earthquakes with much accuracy. However, people have been able to detect and measure earthquakes for a long time. In AD 132, a Chinese philosopher named Zhang Heng built the first earthquake-detecting instrument, or seismoscope, on record. It was a large bronze vessel shaped somewhat like an urn. It had a pendulum hanging inside it that would swing if the earth moved. This pendulum would hit small brass balls that were on the sides of the urn. Where these balls landed indicated the direction and strength of the quake.

The first seismograph was built by Luigi Palmieri in 1856. In 1902 a British scientist named John Milne began setting up a worldwide network of seismographs. By 1913 he had seismographs in 40 locations, including Spain, Syria, Brazil, and Hawaii. Information was sent from each of these locations to Milne's laboratory in England where he was able to compile the information and begin to determine with some accuracy the origin and strength of earthquakes. Today, there are thousands of seismographs around the world. The information gathered at each of these sites is coordinated by the National Earthquake Information Service in Golden, Colorado.

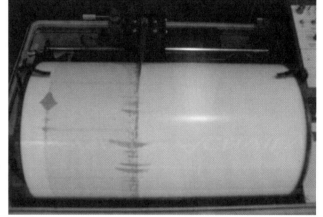

A **seismograph** is an instrument with a large mass attached to a flexible rod. A light attached to the mass traces a line on a rotating drum that is covered with photographic material. If the earth moves, the drum will move with it, but the mass will not move. Some seismographs use pen and paper instead of light and photographic paper; however, the idea is the same.

In 1935 Charles Richter defined the scale that is used to measure the magnitude or strength of an earthquake. The Richter scale is not a linear scale. An earthquake with a magnitude of 3 is 31.6 times stronger than one with a magnitude of 2. A magnitude 4 quake is 31.6 x 31.6 or nearly 1,000 times stronger than a magnitude 2. An earthquake with a magnitude of 5 or greater is considered a serious earthquake, but those with a magnitude of 7 or greater are very strong and usually cause severe damage. The undersea earthquake that caused the tsunami in the Indian Ocean in December 2004 was estimated to be a magnitude of 9.3. The Richter scale uses the distance the seismograph is from the epicenter of the earthquake and the maximum amplitude of the movement of the needle to determine the magnitude of the quake.

The Richter scale is the most important measurement of earthquakes for scientists. However, most people are more concerned about the amount of damage done by an earthquake. So, in 1902 an Italian named Giuseppe Mercalli defined a scale of intensity that describes the amount of damage done by an earthquake. The Mercalli Intensity Scale assigns a number from 1–12 to an earthquake. An earthquake with an intensity of 1 is not felt, an intensity of 4 causes dishes to rattle, an intensity of 9 damages foundations and breaks pipes, and an intensity of 12 causes total destruction.

Collapsed sections of the Cypress viaduct after the 7.1 Loma Prieta earthquake in 1989

The magnitude of an earthquake is only one element determining the destructiveness of an earthquake. The damage done is also dependent on the location of the quake with respect to population, and the length of the tremor. A short earthquake with a large magnitude may not cause as much damage as a longer quake with a smaller magnitude. Buildings can often endure vibration for a few seconds, but cannot stand up under prolonged shaking.

MAKING A SEISMOGRAPH

Purpose: To build your own seismograph

Materials: tape, piece of paper, rolling pin, shoebox, pencil

Procedure:

1. Tape a piece of paper around a rolling pin.

2. Set the rolling pin on top of a shoebox.

3. Have one person slowly rotate the rolling pin while a second person holds a pencil so that the tip touches the paper but the pencil does not touch the shoebox.

4. Have a third person gently shake the box from side to side. Be sure to shake the box in different directions.

5. Observe the marks made on the paper as the box is shaken.

Questions: How does this affect the marks on the paper?

Conclusion: Only movement along the length of the rolling pin will show changes in the markings.

Notice that the bigger the movement of the box, the longer the markings on the paper. An actual seismograph uses paper with special markings showing the Richter scale, making it easier to determine the magnitude of an earthquake.

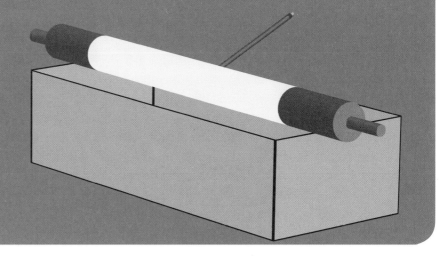

Because accurate prediction of earthquakes could save lives, many scientists continue to gather data and develop models to aid in prediction. The people in Parkfield, California are dedicated to improving earthquake prediction. The people of this small town constantly monitor the earth's movement. The town is filled with seismometers, laser reflectors, magnetometers, strainmeters, and other equipment to detect any changes in the earth in order to learn to how to predict earthquakes.

Despite these efforts, however, all scientists can do today is detect earthquakes as they occur. All prediction methods have proven to be imprecise and unreliable. Only God knows when and where earthquakes will occur. Man has learned to build buildings that are better able to withstand the shock of an earthquake, but he cannot predict the movements of the earth. ■

WHAT DID WE LEARN?

- What is the difference between the magnitude and the intensity of an earthquake?

- What are three factors that determine how much damage is done by an earthquake?

- Explain how a seismograph works.

- What people group was first to record earthquake measurements?

TAKING IT FURTHER

- What are some ways people have learned to prepare for earthquakes?

- What should you do if you are in an earthquake?

EARTHQUAKE LOCATIONS

It is interesting to see where earthquakes happen. If you have access to the Internet, you can do a search to find locations of recent earthquakes. One web site that shows the locations of recent earthquakes is from the U.S. Geological Survey at http://earthquake.usgs.gov/eqcenter/recenteqsww/. Once you have found where the most recent earthquakes have occurred, use an X to mark the locations on your world map. Do you notice any sort of pattern to the location of the earthquakes?

VOLCANOES

Fire mountains

LESSON 24

Why does a volcano erupt?

Words to know:

caldera

active volcano

dormant volcano

extinct volcano

BEGINNERS

We know that earthquakes are caused when the plates in the earth's crust push against each other. This pushing can also cause volcanoes to erupt. When plates rub together they get hot. This causes the rocks deep inside the earth to melt and to build up pressure. This pressure builds up until a channel is found to the surface where it is released as the volcano erupts.

Sometimes there is an earthquake before an eruption and sometimes the volcano erupts without any warning at all. When a volcano erupts, it can be very violent and explosive. Other times, it gently pours the lava out of a hole.

When you think of a volcano erupting, you probably think about lava coming out of it. Lava is melted rock. Most volcanoes shoot out lava, but other things also come out of volcanoes besides lava. Ash and cinders, which are very small and medium-sized bits of rock, can also be found shooting out of volcanoes. You will also see steam and other gases coming out of a volcano. Finally, volcanoes can shoot bombs. A bomb is actually a blob of lava that cools in the air and becomes a solid rock before it hits the ground. All of these things can be very dangerous, so you definitely don't want to be near a volcano when it is erupting.

Some volcanoes are very active. Some rumble and smoke and even erupt continually. Other **active volcanoes** have erupted once and then stopped, but scientists believe that they could erupt again at any time. Some volcanoes are called **dormant volcanoes**. This means that scientists think they are asleep. They have not erupted in the past 50 years, but they could erupt in the future.

Finally, some volcanoes are called **extinct volcanoes**. These are volcanoes that scientists think will not erupt again.

There are hundreds of volcanoes around the world, but most of them are found in countries that circle the Pacific Ocean. Because so many volcanoes are located here, this area around the Pacific Ocean is called the "Ring of Fire."

- What causes a volcano to erupt?

- What is lava?

- What can come out of a volcano besides lava?

- What is the "Ring of Fire"?

Mountains & Movement

Another natural phenomenon closely associated with moving tectonic plates, and often occurring in the same areas of the world as earthquakes, is the eruption of volcanoes. The word *volcano* comes from the name of the Roman god of fire—Vulcan. *Volcano* can refer to the hole that lava comes out of and also to the mountain formed by that lava.

It is believed that friction between the moving plates allows the mantle to grow hotter. When the magma heats up, it expands and when the pressure builds up, the result is often a volcanic eruption. Magma, melted rock that is 30–120 miles (50–195 km) below the earth's surface, expands until it finds a vent or channel through the crust to the surface of the earth. Magma that reaches the surface is called lava.

Volcanoes can erupt very suddenly and violently, or they can gently pour out their contents relatively quietly. Sometimes the pressures within a volcano cause earthquakes prior to an eruption, and other times an eruption occurs without any warning at all. Volcanoes can emit any or all of the following:

- Lava—liquid melted rock, with temperatures from 1,300–2,200ºF (700–1,200ºC). Lava can rush downhill at speeds up to 35 mph (15.6 m/s).

- Ash—tiny fragments of solid rock, less than 0.2 inches (0.5 cm) in diameter

- Cinders—larger fragments of solid rock, 0.2–1 inch (0.5–2.5 cm) in diameter

- Bombs—blobs of lava that solidify in the air and hit the earth as rock

- Gases—many gases are dissolved in the magma. These often separate from the magma as it approaches the surface. So steam, carbon dioxide, and other gases often shoot out of a volcano. Steam quickly condenses as it hits the cool atmosphere, and sometimes this water mixing with the soil can cause severe mudslides.

Lava, ash, and mud harden as they cool and form mountains around the exit of the volcano. Although these mountains can take different shapes and forms, the basic structure of all volcanoes is the same. A volcano has a magma chamber under the earth's crust. It has a central vent, which is a

FUN FACT

Mount Rainier, the highest peak in Washington state, is a volcano that still steams, but it last erupted in the 1800s.

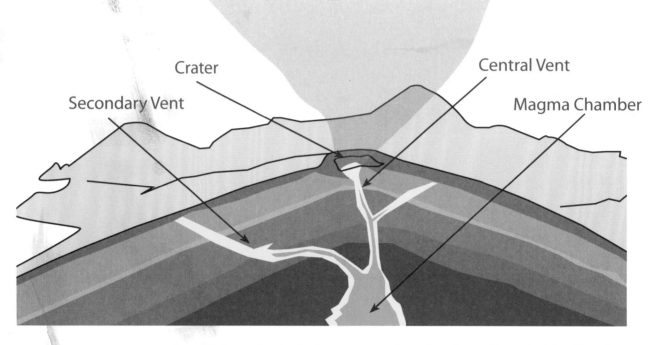

Crater

Secondary Vent

Central Vent

Magma Chamber

tube or channel through which the magma is forced to the surface. And finally, it has a crater, sometimes called a caldera, which is a bowl-shaped depression around the mouth of the volcano. This crater forms when a cone that was formed at the mouth of the volcano by the cooling lava later collapses. Some very active volcanoes sometimes develop secondary vents through which the magma may also escape.

Volcanoes are classified by their activity into one of three categories. Active volcanoes are ones that have erupted at least once in the past 50 years. Dormant volcanoes are ones that have not erupted in the past 50 years but are expected to

VOLCANO MODEL

Purpose: To make a model of a volcano

Materials: empty bottle, baking sheet, baking soda, newspaper, vinegar, red food coloring

Procedure:

1. Place an empty bottle in the center of a baking sheet or other tray with sides.

2. Pour one teaspoon of baking soda into the bottle.

3. Crunch up newspaper and place it around the bottle to

form a mountain with the bottle in the center and tape the paper to the bottle. (The only part of the bottle that should be visible is the mouth of the bottle. Be sure all paper is on the baking sheet and not hanging over the edge.)

4. Pour ½ cup of vinegar into a measuring cup and add a few drops of red food coloring.

5. Pour the vinegar into the bottle and watch your volcano erupt!

Be sure to clean up your mess when you are done.

Conclusion: The bottle represents the magma chamber under the newspaper crust. The mouth of the bottle is the vent. Although we are not heating the "lava," the reaction between the baking soda and the vinegar produces carbon dioxide gas that expands and finds its way out of the bottle "volcano," just like heated magma in a real volcano.

erupt in the future. **Extinct volcanoes** are ones that have not erupted in the past 50 years and are not expected to erupt again in the foreseeable future. Volcanoes may be very active, erupting over and over again, and then suddenly stop and remain dormant for hundreds or possibly even thousands of years. Classifying a volcano as extinct is tricky. Some volcanoes that were believed to be extinct have suddenly and unexpectedly come back to life.

More than 500 active volcanoes exist today. Most of these are found along an area called the "Ring of Fire," an area encircling the Pacific Ocean. More than 125 of these active volcanoes are in the island country of Indonesia. It is estimated that there have been about 1,300 active volcanoes in the past several thousand years.

Not all volcanoes form on land. Many volcanoes form under the ocean. We often don't see evidence of their existence unless they get high enough to form islands. The Hawaiian Islands were formed by underwater volcanoes. ■

WHAT DID WE LEARN?

- What are the three stages or states of a volcano?
- Describe the three main parts of a volcano.
- Give the name for each of the following items that is emitted from a volcano:
  1. Liquid or melted rock
  2. Tiny bits of solid rock
  3. Pieces of rock from 0.2 to 1 inch (0.5–2.5 cm) in diameter
  4. Blobs of lava that solidify in the air
  5. Steam and carbon dioxide

TAKING IT FURTHER

- How might a volcano become active without anyone noticing?
- How are volcanoes and earthquakes related?
- How certain can we be that a volcano is really extinct?

VOLCANO LOCATIONS

Today you are going to finish your world map by adding some of the more famous volcanoes to your map. Draw a small smoking mountain in each location and label each of the following volcanoes on your map. Use a world atlas or the Internet to help you locate each volcano, if necessary.

- Mount St. Helens— Washington state

- Mt. Vesuvius—Italy
- Mauna Loa—Hawaii
- Krakatoa—Indonesia
- Mt. Pinatubo—Philippines
- Mt. Etna—Sicily
- Mt. Fuji—Japan
- Kilauea—Hawaii
- Akutan—Aleutian Islands (near Alaska)

- Santa Maria—Guatemala
- Mount Erebus—Antarctica
- Bezymianny Volcano— Kamchatka, Russia

Do you notice a pattern to the locations of these volcanoes? Most of them are located around the edge of the Pacific Ocean. This is called the "Ring of Fire" for a good reason.

MT. VESUVIUS

Smoke, ash, choking fire, and mothers dying in an effort to protect their children. These scenes are forever recorded in the stones, mud, and ash that covered the city of Pompeii during the destructive eruption of Mt. Vesuvius in AD 79. But that wasn't the first time Mt. Vesuvius had erupted, nor would it be the last. The volcano was recorded by both Greek and Roman scholars and was known to have destroyed many small towns around it before that time. So why is this eruption so famous? First, it is famous because of the way the volcano covered the towns of Herculaneum and Pompeii, and second, because of the eyewitness account of the eruption.

A young man called Pliny the Younger, who lived from AD 61–113, recorded the account of this event. He was about 18 years old when this event took place. At the time, his uncle Pliny the Elder was commander of the Roman fleet at Misenum. Misenum was across the Bay of Naples from Pompeii, a distance of about 25 miles (40 km). On the afternoon of August 24, AD 79, Pliny the Younger's mother drew Pliny the Elder's attention to an unusual cloud. Pliny the Elder climbed up to where he could get a better view of the cloud. The cloud was described as pine tree shaped with a long trunk. It appeared to rise out of one of the mountains,

but he could not tell which one. Some of the cloud was white while other parts of it were dark like patches of dirt or ash. Having a scientific bent, he was determined to get a closer look at this unusual sight.

He ordered his boat to be made ready and asked if Pliny the Younger wanted to go along. The boy chose to stay behind and study. As he was about to leave, Pliny the Elder received a letter from Tascius's wife Rectina. She said she was terrified. Her villa lay at the foot of Mt. Vesuvius and she had no way out of Pompeii except by boat. She wanted Pliny to send a boat for her. Historians are not sure who she was, but she must have been important to Pliny. Instead of just investigating the smoke cloud, he decided to launch the quadriremes, all of the boats under his command. He then hurried into the face of danger, to a place others were fleeing, to save as many people as he could. He did not show his fear if he had any. As he traveled toward Pompeii, he continued his observations of the volcano, dictating what he saw.

As the boats got closer, more and more ash and rocks began falling on them. His helmsman urged him to turn back, but he said, "Fortune helps the brave, head for Pomponianus." A good wind made it easy for his boats to put in near Pompeii, but it also made it impossible for his boats, or any of the other boats, to leave at that time. Upon his arrival, he gave comfort and courage to Pomponianus, one of the other ship owners. To help lessen the fear around him, he asked to be taken to the baths where he relaxed. Later he dined with friends.

As night came on, it became more apparent that flames were lighting up different parts of Vesuvius. To calm people down, he said the flames were from the deserted homes of those who left in a hurry with hearth fires still going. He then rested for the night. It was said that those who passed his door that night heard him snoring. During the night, stones and ash built up against his door, and if he had slept any longer he would not have made it out of his room.

He decided to try for the open sea but when he got down to his boat he found the weather to be as rough and uncooperative as before. He sat down to drink some water, and then upon standing, he collapsed. The exact cause of his death is unknown. It is not known if any of his boats made it out of the harbor, but someone survived in order to relay his account which was recorded by his nephew, Pliny the Younger.

The city of Pompeii was covered with cinders and ash and was unseen for at least 1,500 years. Because the city was quickly covered with ash, much of the city was preserved. The ruins that have been uncovered in the last 50 years give us a very complete picture of what Roman life was like. Herculaneum was also covered at the same time, but instead of being covered with ash, it was covered with mud, which did much damage, making it more difficult to uncover.

Over the years, Mt. Vesuvius has continued to be very active. Since that day in AD 79, Mt. Vesuvius has had at least 28 other major eruptions. But because of Pliny's eyewitness account, and the many artifacts uncovered in Pompeii, the eruption of AD 79 remains the most famous.

VOLCANO TYPES

Is there more than one?

What are the different types of volcanoes?

Words to know:

shield volcano

cinder cone

composite volcano

geothermal

Challenge words:

andesitic volcano

basaltic volcano

BEGINNERS

Volcanoes form mountains as they send out lava, ash, and cinders. Different volcanoes form different shaped mountains depending on what is coming out of the volcano. If a volcano shoots out mostly lava, it forms a rounded mountain. This type of volcano is called a **shield volcano** because it looks a little like a giant shield lying on the ground.

If a volcano shoots out mostly ash and cinders and very little lava, then it forms a mountain that has steep sides. This is called a **cinder cone**. Cinder cone volcanoes are usually not as tall as other volcanoes.

Most volcanoes are not shield volcanoes or cinder cones. Most volcanoes shoot out lava for a while, then shoot out ash and cinders for a while, then more lava. When a volcano alternates between lava and solid materials it forms a mountain called a **composite volcano**. Composite volcanoes form mountains that are cone-shaped. Mount Fuji and Mount St. Helens are two famous composite volcanoes.

- What kind of mountain is formed when mostly lava comes from a volcano?

- What kind of mountain is formed when mostly ash and cinders come from a volcano?

- What kind of mountain is formed when a volcano alternates between lava and solid material?

What is the first thing you think of when you hear the word volcano? Is it lava? Lava is a very important component of volcanoes. There are two kinds of lava that can flow from a volcano. The first kind, aa (pronounced "ah-ah"), carries sharp chunks of rock called *scoria*. Aa cools very quickly and builds up quickly. The second type of lava is pahoehoe (pronounced "pa-hoy-hoy"). This type of lava forms a smooth skin on top, allowing the hot lava to flow beneath it. It is usually about three feet (1 m) thick and cools into ropy patterns. Some volcanoes pour out lava in a more or less continuous flow. Other eruptions are very explosive—sometimes blowing the top off of the mountain.

The types and amount of lava flowing from a volcano determine its shape. Although all volcanoes have the same basic internal structure, all volcanoes do not have the same external shape. The shape of the mountain formed by the volcano differs according to what is emitted from the volcano.

A **shield volcano** has gently sloping sides. A shield volcano is formed when mostly lava is emitted. Shield volcanoes are usually found in areas where tectonic plates are

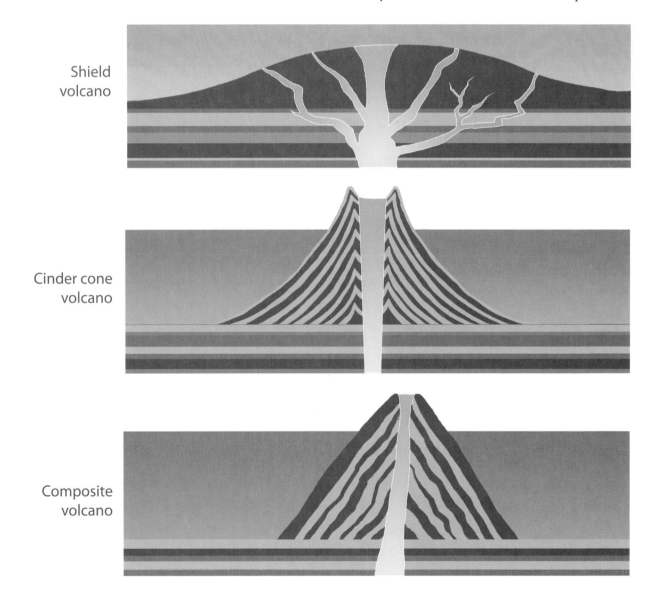

Shield volcano

Cinder cone volcano

Composite volcano

moving apart instead of rubbing against each other. Mauna Loa and Mauna Kea, both part of the Hawaiian Islands, are examples of shield volcanoes.

Cinder cones are formed when a volcano emits mostly ashes, cinders, and bombs. Cinder cones have steep sloping sides and are usually smaller than other types of volcanoes. Paricutin, a volcano that suddenly formed in the middle of a farm in Mexico, is an example of a cinder cone volcano.

Most volcanoes, however, are **composite volcanoes**. These are formed when a volcano alternates between emitting mostly lava and mostly solid material. Composite volcanoes usually have a symmetrical cone shape. Composite volcanoes are most often found near subduction zones, areas where one plate is sliding under another. Mount Fuji, Mount St. Helens, and Mount Vesuvius are all examples of composite volcanoes.

Although volcanoes can be extremely dangerous and destructive, they have many beneficial side effects. The ash and other chemicals enrich the soil. Volcanic soil is very fertile. Also, many volcanic areas have large deposits of sulfur, which is needed in the manufacturing of rubber and fertilizers. Volcanoes offer a source of **geothermal** (heat) energy. Hot vents near underwater volcanoes create unique ecosystems in the ocean. Some species of plants and animals can only survive near these vents. And finally, volcanoes form new land.

One of the most beautiful results of volcanic eruptions is the black sand beaches of Hawaii. Black sand is formed when hot lava hits the cool seawater and shatters into tiny crystals. It is black because of the high amount of iron oxide in the lava.

Some of the more famous volcanoes include:

- Mount Vesuvius, Italy—Erupted in AD 79, completely covering the cities of Herculaneum and Pompeii with 20 feet (6 m) of ash and mud. It has erupted several times since then.

- Kilauea, Hawaii—Has been continually erupting since 1983, causing the island of Hawaii to continue to grow.

COOL VOLCANO

Purpose: To create a delicious ice cream volcano

Materials: half gallon ice cream, pie pan, chocolate syrup, cookie crumbs, chocolate chips

Procedure:

1. Allow a half gallon of ice cream to soften slightly.

2. Place the ice cream in a pie pan and shape it into your favorite volcano shape.

3. Place it in the freezer for about four hours.

4. Remove it from the freezer and scoop out a crater.

5. Fill the crater with chocolate syrup "lava" and allow it to flow down the sides.

6. Decorate it with cookie crumb ash and chocolate chip bombs. Why not take a picture of the masterpiece before you enjoy eating your cool volcano?

- Mount Pinatubo, Philippines—Erupted in June 1991. The amount of ash put into the atmosphere is credited with lowering the temperature around the world that year.

- Krakatoa, Indonesia—Erupted in 1883. It is one of the largest eruptions in recorded history. The ash and rocks created huge tsunamis. ■

WHAT DID WE LEARN?

- What are the three shapes of volcanoes, and how is each formed?

- Where are most active volcanoes located today?

- What are some of the dangers of volcanoes?

- What are some positive side effects of volcanoes?

TAKING IT FURTHER

- How is the formation of black sand beaches different from the formation of white sand beaches?

VOLCANOES AND TECTONICS

The type of volcano that forms in a particular area is often related to what is happening with nearby tectonic plates. In areas where subduction is occurring, the volcanoes that form are usually composite volcanoes. They are also called **andesitic volcanoes**. The sides of these volcanoes are steep because the lava is slow moving and cools before it flows very far. Often the lava and ash will build up inside the vent of the volcano and can eventually plug the opening. When this happens, pressure can build up until there is a violent explosion. Most of the volcanoes in the Ring of Fire are andesitic volcanoes.

When tectonic plates are moving apart, a different kind of volcano can form above the rift. These volcanoes are called **basaltic volcanoes** and form shield-shaped mountains. The lava from a basaltic volcano is made of basalt and is usually very runny and flows very fast. It can flow for long distances before it hardens into rock. This is why basaltic volcanoes form mountains with gently sloping sides instead of forming steep mountains. Most basaltic volcanoes are found in the middle of the oceans and most of them are below the surface of the ocean. The islands of Hawaii were formed by basaltic volcanoes.

For a fun experiment, with your parent's permission, take an unopened can of soda outside, shake it up for about 15 seconds, then hold it so that the opening is facing away from you and anyone else around you, and quickly pop the can open. Shaking the can causes pressure to build up inside the can just as moving tectonic plates cause pressure to build up inside the earth. Opening the can releases the pressure and allows the contents to come shooting out. This is what happens when lava and hot gases find a vent through the earth's crust and come shooting out.

MOUNT ST. HELENS

God's gift to scientists

LESSON

26

What can we learn from the eruption of Mount St. Helens?

BEGINNERS

One of the most famous volcanoes in the United States is Mount St. Helens, located in southwest Washington state. Mount St. Helens had been quiet for 123 years, but on May 18, 1980, it erupted with a huge explosion. The explosion blew 1,300 feet (400 m) off the top of the mountain. It was as powerful as 33,000 atomic bombs. The explosion was heard 200 miles (320 km) away. This was an awesome and frightening eruption.

Although the eruption of a volcano can be frightening, it can also be very interesting. Scientists were able to watch everything that happened around the volcano and have learned many things that they did not know before.

One interesting thing that happened was that the ash and debris from the explosion settled to form layers that grew 25 feet (7.6 m) high in only one day. These layers look very much like areas of sedimentary rock found in other parts of the world. So it looks like much of the sedimentary rock we have today could have been formed rapidly as a result of volcanic activity in the past associated with Noah's Flood.

Another interesting thing that happened near Mount St. Helens was that a huge amount of mud and water flowed out of the volcano and carved a large canyon that was 100 feet (30.5 m) deep through the layers of fresh rock nearby. It did not take millions of years for that canyon to form; it only took a lot of mud and water and a very short period of time. Many scientists believe that Grand Canyon was formed by a lot of water and a little time, too.

Studying what happened during and after the eruption of Mount St. Helens has shown scientists that a large natural disaster can result in many of the things that we see around us. This helps to support what the Bible says about the age of the earth and what happened during the Flood of Noah's time.

- **What happened at Mount St. Helens on May 18, 1980?**

- **How long did it take for 25 feet of layered ash to accumulate after the eruption?**

- **What did the flood of mud and water from the volcano do?**

Mountains & Movement

At 8:32 a.m., on May 18, 1980, after being quiet for 123 years, Mount St. Helens, in southwest Washington state, suddenly burst into life. The explosion that blew off the north side of the mountain was heard up to 200 miles (320 km) away. The summit was lowered by 1,300 feet (400 m), as rock was blown off. The avalanche of rock was followed by a flow of hot gas and ash rushing down the side of the mountain. The explosions lasted for nine hours. Millions of tons of ash were shot 15 miles (24 km) into the atmosphere. Ash darkened the skies around the world for two months. The energy released by this eruption was equal to that of 33,000 atomic bombs, or 400 million tons of dynamite. There had been small earthquakes in the area for two months before the eruption, but no one expected the explosive display that occurred.

The eruption of Mount St. Helens was a frightening event, but it was exciting as well. Many consider it a gift to scientists, since it has given us much scientific knowledge that could not be gained anywhere else. Much of the data collected at Mount St. Helens reveals how catastrophes such as Noah's Flood can explain much of the geology we see today.

Formation of sedimentary rock

When an evolutionist looks at sedimentary rock with hundreds of thin layers, he believes that the layers were deposited slowly over millions of years. However, the eruption of Mount St. Helens deposited over 25 feet (7.6 m) of debris, mostly composed of thin layers of ash, in only one day! There is evidence that there was extensive volcanic activity associated with the Genesis Flood. This activity could account for much of the sedimentary rock formations we see today. Mount St. Helens showed us that these formations can form very quickly as a result of a catastrophe, instead of slowly over millions of years.

FUN FACT

In the 1880s a volcanic eruption in New Zealand buried a village. Sixty years later a fossilized hat, a fossilized bag of flour, and a fossilized ham were dug up. Fossils do not require millions of years to form!

Ash from Mount St. Helens darkened the sky around the world. The 1815 eruption of Tambora in Indonesia spewed millions of tons of ash into the atmosphere. The following year, the New England states, Canada, England, and France all experienced snow in June and frost in July as a result of that eruption. It is therefore likely that the massive amounts of ash put into the atmosphere due to volcanic activity at the time of the Flood contributed greatly to the cooler summers needed to form the great Ice Age.

Formation of canyons

Another evolutionary idea that has been challenged by Mount St. Helens is the idea that canyons are formed by millions of years of erosion from the rivers flowing through them. Mudflows from the eruption of Mount St. Helens carved a canyon 100 feet (30 m) high and 100 feet (30 m) wide through solid rock in only one day! This canyon has been nicknamed "Little Grand Canyon." This event is forcing scientists to rethink how the actual Grand Canyon may have been formed. Creation scientists believe that the canyon was made by a huge amount of water in a short period of time—not by a small amount of water over a long period of time.

Spirit Lake

Spirit Lake is located at the foot of Mount St. Helens, and some very fascinating things are happening there. First, a whole forest of trees was wiped out by the blast. After the blast more than 10,000 logs were floating on Spirit Lake, and as they became waterlogged they began floating upright, with their roots pointing down. After only ten years these logs began to

Mudflows following the eruption of Mount St. Helens formed a canyon from solid rock in only one day.

Floating logs on Spirit Lake

VOLCANO WORD SEARCH

Using a copy of the "Volcano Word Search," review the meaning of each word as you find it in the puzzle.

settle into the layers of sediment at the bottom of the lake, many of them settling upright with their roots on the bottom of the lake. This may explain how many fossilized tree trunks became fossilized in a vertical position through many layers of sediment. Evolutionists have not been able to adequately explain these formations, called *petrified forests*, with millions of years of slow deposition. A similar formation called Specimen Ridge, in Yellowstone National Park, had been interpreted by evolutionists to show 50 million years of activity, but Mount St. Helens showed that one catastrophe could account for this type of formation in only a few years. (See also www.answersingenesis.org/go/yellowstone.)

As scientists continue to study the area around Mount St. Helens, they are finding more and more evidence that catastrophic processes can account for much of what evolutionists have claimed requires millions of years to form. Scientific evidence confirms the Bible's history. (For more information on Mount St. Helens and how it supports the biblical accounts of Creation and the Flood, see www.answersingenesis.org/go/helens.) ■

WHAT DID WE LEARN?

- Describe some of the ways the data collected at Mount St. Helens is challenging evolutionary thinking.

TAKING IT FURTHER

- How did the ash from the eruption of Mount St. Helens affect the weather in 1980?
- How could volcanic activity have contributed to the onset of the Ice Age?

PREDICTING ERUPTIONS

Mount St. Helens began erupting again in September, 2004. However, this eruption was very different from the explosive eruption of 1980. The eruption began with small earthquakes and steam coming from the vent of the volcano. Lava began pouring into the crater on October 10, 2004. Since that time a lava dome has been growing inside the crater. Scientists do not know when this current eruption will stop.

Because 57 people died in the 1980 eruption, it would be nice if scientists could predict another violent eruption before it happens. However, volcanoes are unpredictable right now. In order to gain better understanding of what is going on underneath the volcano, scientists have placed 17 sensors around the mountain in hopes of detecting movement that might lead to an explosion.

Some of the instruments are placed in 6-inch (15-centimeter) wide, 800-feet (244-meter) deep holes in various locations around the crater. The instruments include strainmeters to detect tiny amounts of ground deformation, which could indicate pressure or strain in the rocks, and tiltmeters to help detect any movement of the rocks. A global positioning satellite (GPS) system consisting of nine GPS units is connected to the system to detect any movement of the ground on the surface. All of the sensors are connected to a computer system in Boulder, Colorado, where scientists can view and analyze the data in the hopes of predicting future volcanic eruptions.

UNIT 4

WATER
& EROSION

Geysers

Heated ground water

LESSON
27

What is a geyser and how does it work?

Words to know:

geyser

hot spring

spouter

fumarole

mud pot

BEGINNERS

Have you ever heard of Old Faithful? It is a geyser in Yellowstone National Park. A **geyser** is an opening in the ground where hot water and steam shoots out. Old Faithful got its name from the fact that water and steam shoot out of it about once every 90 minutes, 24 hours a day, 365 days a year. That's pretty faithful.

In just a few places around the world, magma, which is melted rock under the ground, is close enough to the surface to heat water that is in the ground. When the water gets hot, it expands and takes up more room. This creates pressure under the ground. The water will move up until it finds an opening in the ground. If the pressure is great enough, the water will shoot out of the ground in a huge fountain. This is a geyser.

Once the geyser has erupted, the ground will fill with water again and it will eventually erupt again when the pressure underground becomes great enough. Some geysers like Old Faithful erupt frequently. Other geysers only erupt once in a while, and their eruptions cannot be predicted.

If water is heated underground but it can find a way out without much pressure building up, it will form a **hot spring**. The hot water will bubble up into a pool. Sometimes a hot spring will contain more dirt than water and it becomes a **mud pot**.

Often, minerals from the rocks underground become dissolved in the hot water and are carried to the surface of the earth. When the water evaporates, the

minerals are left behind. These mineral deposits can form beautiful rock formations. If you have a chance to visit Yellowstone National Park in Wyoming, you
can see all of these wonderful creations.

- What causes a geyser to erupt?

- How is a hot spring different from a geyser?

- Where can you see many geysers?

Old Faithful is probably the most famous geyser in the world. Anyone
who has been to Yellowstone National Park has most likely been able
to observe the majestic spray of the hot water shooting into the sky.
But many people do not realize that this phenomenon is closely associated with volcanoes and earthquakes.

Geysers are a result of heated ground water. Underground water can be heated
one of two ways. Scientists have observed that the interior temperature of the earth
rises about 87°F (30.5°C) per mile. This is called the thermal gradient of the earth.
So, as water seeps deeper into the earth, its temperature becomes hotter and hotter.
The second way that water is heated is by magma rising closer to the surface. As the
magma rises, it heats the rocks and water around it. Magma most frequently rises to
the surface near joints in the tectonic plates.

Just like air, hot water rises and cold water sinks. This property causes geysers
as well as many other interesting phenomena. The most common manifestation of
heated ground water is a hot spring. In a spring, heated water rises or bubbles to the
surface. Springs are relatively calm. Spouters are more active hot pools. In a spouter,
water continually bubbles and gives off steam. Sometimes the water is superheated
and reaches the earth's surface as steam only. This is called a fumarole, or steam vent.
Fumaroles can sometimes be very noisy as the steam pushes its way to the surface.
Heated ground water often contains hydrogen sulfide, giving the pools and springs
the smell of rotten eggs.

Different temperatures of water promote growth of different algae and bacteria
resulting in myriad colors in hot springs. The colors can change from the center of
the pool to the edges as the cooling
water spreads out. Many hot springs
have a rainbow appearance.

If a hot spring contains more dirt
than water, it becomes a mud pot
(shown here). Steam bubbles to the
surface and spatters out. Often the
dirt in mud pots contains minerals
that make the mud different colors.
These mud pots are often called
paint pots and can make a beautiful
display. Occasionally, a mud pot
forms a cone that can become

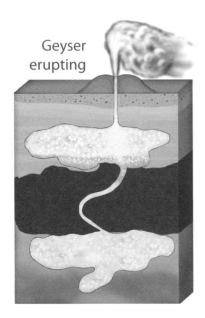

Geyser
erupting

Underground chambers
filling with water

clogged. When this happens, pressure builds until mud and steam erupt out of the top. This is called a *mud volcano*. It is a similar phenomenon to an actual volcano, but mud volcanoes are usually very small compared to lava volcanoes.

Finally, the most spectacular display of heated water is the geyser. Hot water erupts from underneath the ground and can shoot hundreds of feet into the air. Geysers form where rock containing ground water in long twisting chambers is heated by magma which lies as little as 2 to 5 miles (3.2–8 km) below the surface. The water is heated to as much as 400°F (205°C). This super-heated water expands and builds up pressure. When the pressure of the super-heated water becomes greater than the weight of the water above it, the water is forced through a vent leading from the underground chambers to the surface. After an eruption, the chambers begin to refill with water and the process starts over.

Some geysers such as Old Faithful erupt regularly, more or less on a schedule. In 1970 Old Faithful was erupting about every 66 minutes. By 2000 it was erupting about every 77 minutes. Some people are concerned that Old Faithful is losing its power since its eruption times are becoming further apart.

Other geysers erupt irregularly and their eruptions cannot be predicted. Irregular geysers occur because their underground plumbing is shared with other pools or geysers. For example, sometimes another geyser in Yellowstone, Daisy Geyser, erupts for about three minutes every 1½ to 3 hours while Bonita Pool quietly overflows. At other times, Bonita overflows heavily with small eruptions and Daisy erupts very seldom. These two geysers share the same underground water system, thus preventing Daisy from erupting consistently.

Water from hot springs often dissolves minerals from the rocks through which it flows. Then, after it reaches the surface and evaporates, the minerals are left behind. Geysers often form or leave behind mounds of geyserite—a material made from silica. You can find another beautiful example of mineral deposits left by heated water in Yellowstone at Mammoth Hot Springs (pictured at left). Here beautiful terraces of travertine, or calcium carbonate, have been left behind as the water flows down the hillside. The basic color of the terraces is white but the edges display a rainbow of colors as the different temperatures of water encourage the growth of algae and bacteria in various shades of brown, green, red, yellow, and blue.

Terraces at Mammoth Hot Springs

The heated water in areas such as Yellowstone provides unique habitats for animals and plants that would not normally live in the area. Some fish can live in water as hot as 104°F (40°C), and may be able to tolerate temperatures as high as 110°F (43°C) for a few minutes. Even with an ability to live in such warm water, the fish still can't live too close to the hot springs, but must live downstream from the source of heat.

Also, in the dead of winter when most areas are free of insects, flies live near the hot springs. They fly up and down near the hot springs trying to keep their body temperatures just right. If they move even a few feet away from the spring they will die in minutes.

This same heat can also keep small protected pockets of grass, mosses, and flowers alive all winter. Some flowers can even bloom in the middle of winter due to the heat.

Half of all the geysers in the world are found in Yellowstone National Park. Nearly all geysers are found in only four places: Yellowstone, Kronotski National Park in Russia, North Island in New Zealand, and Iceland. ■

MAKE A GEYSER

Purpose: To make a geyser

Materials: cup, soda straw

Procedure:

1. Fill a cup with water and take it and a soda straw outside.

2. Fill the straw with water and hold your finger over the end of the straw to prevent the water from spilling out.

3. Place the other end of the straw in your mouth and point the straw up in the air and blow out the water. You have made your own geyser!

4. Refill the straw with water and repeat.

Conclusion: The straw represents the underground plumbing that fills up with water. The air from your lungs represents the pressure produced when the heated water expands. Refilling the straw and repeating represents what happens with many geysers such as Old Faithful, as water refills the underground chambers.

WHAT DID WE LEARN?

- What are some ways that heated ground water shows up on the surface of the earth?

- Explain how a geyser works.

- How is a mud pot different from a hot spring?

TAKING IT FURTHER

- How might a scientist figure out which irregular geysers are connected underground?

- Why do some hot pools have a rainbow appearance?

- Can you tell the temperature of the water just by looking at a pool?

GEOTHERMAL ENERGY

Geysers, fumaroles, and hot springs are all associated with volcanic activity. Even though there may not be any active volcanoes in the area, magma is closer to the surface in areas with these features than in other parts of the earth. The magma heats the groundwater, turning it into steam. This creates a unique opportunity for generating electricity. Steam is used in power plants to turn the turbines that generate electricity, so power plants have been built in many of these areas to take advantage of the naturally occurring steam.

Geothermal energy is used in many places around the world, mostly near the edges of tectonic plates. In Iceland, over 80% of all homes are heated with geothermal energy. Geothermal power plants have also been built in the United States, New Zealand, Japan, China, Africa, and Europe.

One area north of San Francisco, California, is called The Geysers. Although there are no actual geysers in this area, there are abundant hot pools and fumaroles, indicating that magma is close to the surface. The first power plant was built at The Geysers in 1955 and today the power plant produces enough electricity for 750,000 homes.

To understand how this power plant works, you first need to understand the geology of the area. Magma is only a few miles below the surface of the earth. This magma heats the rocks around it and as water seeps into the ground above, it is heated as well. Above the area with the ground water is an area of hard rock that traps the underground heated water. This causes the water and steam to build up pressure below ground.

Holes have been drilled two miles deep through the cap rock into the rock containing the steam. These holes act like drinking straws, drawing the steam up out of the ground. The steam is then passed through a filter to remove any impurities, and then it is used to turn the turbines. After passing through the turbines, the steam is cooled and the water is returned to the ground. Approximately 25% of the water taken from the ground is recycled and the rest is lost to evaporation. This is a very efficient way to generate electricity since it does not require the burning of any other fuel to turn water into steam.

Areas with geothermal power plants must have trapped steam, but do not necessarily have geysers. A geothermal power plant was built in North Island, New Zealand where there were many geysers. There used to be 200 active geysers, but today there are only 12 active geysers. This is partially due to the building of power plants and partially due to earthquakes that have changed the underground plumbing of the area. However, because steam is still available, the power plant still works.

Questions:

- Why are geothermal power plants mostly located near edges of tectonic plates?

- Would you expect geothermal power plants to experience more or fewer earthquakes than other power plants?

- Why is geothermal energy considered a renewable resource?

WEATHERING & EROSION

It's wearing me down

What causes weathering and erosion?

Words to know:

weathering

erosion

frost heaving

Challenge words:

oxidation

BEGINNERS

When rocks are broken apart into smaller pieces by wind, rain, and other things it is called **weathering** or **erosion**. The rocks are worn away a little at a time. This can happen in many ways. One way that rocks can be broken is by water. When rain falls against rocks, it can break away tiny bits of the rock. Sometimes water fills in small cracks in a rock. When the water freezes it expands, or takes up more space. The ice then pushes on the rock and makes the crack bigger. As the crack fills with more water and freezes, the crack gets even bigger. Eventually, the rock will break apart.

Wind can also cause rocks to break into pieces. Wind blows bits of rock, glass, and other materials against rocks, breaking off tiny pieces of rock. Strong winds can eventually wear away large amounts of rock.

Although wind and water are the main ways that rocks are worn down or broken, they are not the only ways. As plants grow, their roots get longer. These roots push through the soil and sometimes push through cracks in rocks breaking them apart.

Finally, chemicals can react with certain rocks to wear away the rock surface. These chemicals get into the soil when plants decay and get into the air from pollution. When these chemicals come in contact with certain rocks, they wear away some of the rock.

Erosion is constantly happening around us. It usually happens slowly. Usually only tiny bits of rock are worn away at a time, but after a long time, you can see a difference in the surface of the earth. Sometimes erosion happens very quickly. When there is a flood, the water can wear away a huge amount of rock at one time.

- **What is erosion?**

- **What happens to a rock when water freezes inside a crack?**

- **What are three ways that rocks can be eroded?**

- **Does erosion happen slowly or quickly?**

The second law of thermodynamics says that all systems tend toward maximum entropy or total disorder. The Bible says in Psalm 102:25–26, "Of old You laid the foundation of the earth, And the heavens are the work of Your hands. They will perish, but You will endure; Yes, they will all grow old like a garment. . . ." Contrary to evolutionary claims that there is a continuous change toward higher life forms and increased order, what we actually observe are destruction, extinction, and loss of energy. We can easily observe that the surface of the earth is wearing out just by observing the rocks and hills. The surface wears away through three different processes: weathering, mass wasting, and stream erosion. We will discuss weathering in this lesson and the other processes in the following lessons.

Weathering, or erosion, is the natural process of wearing down and breaking apart rocks. Rocks can be broken down by either chemical or mechanical means. The most common form of chemical erosion takes place when certain minerals react chemically with acids. Limestone, in particular, dissolves quickly when it comes in contact with acids. Two commonly occurring acids are carbonic acid and humic acid. Carbon dioxide mixes with water to form carbonic acid, and decaying plants produce humic acid. These weak acids chemically dissolve many of the rocks they come in contact with.

Mechanical weathering is the second means by which rocks can be worn away. Different forces break off pieces of rock or even crack huge rocks apart. Water is the main mechanical force that breaks up rocks. Water fills small cracks in rocks. When it freezes, water expands about 8%, thus increasing the size of the crack and

⌕ WEATHERING AT WORK

To observe different types of weathering, perform the experiments and answer the questions on the "Weathering" worksheet.

forcing small bits of rock to break off. After the water melts, more water can enter the larger crack. When this freezes, the crack is again enlarged. After many cycles, the water and ice eventually break the rock apart.

This freezing/thawing cycle also occurs underground. The expanding water can push rocks upward. The melting ice allows loose soil to fill in under the rock. The next freezing cycle pushes the rock up further. This process is called **frost heaving**. Rocks can be pushed to the surface from as much as 18 inches (45 cm) below ground each winter. Farmers must deal with new rocks in their fields each spring because of this process.

A third mechanical weathering force is one you might not expect. Plant and tree roots can place continuing pressure on rocks and can force cracks to expand and rocks to break apart.

Finally, wind is a strong mechanical weathering agent. Strong winds can blow debris against rock faces, breaking off bits of rock. This results in many beautiful rock formations but can also ruin the paint on the side of your car or wear away the words on a sign. Weathering forces are constantly at work on the surface of the earth, wearing down the rocks and changing the face of the planet. ■

WHAT DID WE LEARN?

- What is weathering?
- Describe the two types of weathering.

TAKING IT FURTHER

- How does freezing and thawing of water break rocks?
- What do people do that is similar to mechanical weathering?

CHEMICAL EROSION

There are many types of chemical erosion. You have already learned about acids that can erode various materials. But water is also a chemical eroding agent. Many substances can be dissolved in water and thus eroded away as water flows over the soil and rocks. Oxygen also contributes to chemical erosion. Many metals,

especially iron, react with oxygen. This is called *oxidation*.

When iron combines with oxygen it is called *rusting*. Rust is much weaker than iron so it is more easily eroded. Thus, when oxidation occurs it increases the rate at which erosion takes place. The rate of oxidation is affected by the amount of water available

as well. Rusting happens more quickly in a humid environment than in a dry environment.

Complete the experiment described on the "Chemical Erosion" worksheet. This demonstrates the effects of rust on iron and the effects of humidity on rust rates. Soil and rocks in many areas are worn away because of oxidation.

MASS WASTING

The force of gravity

How does gravity cause erosion?

Words to know:

mass wasting

creep

landslide

avalanche

Challenge words:

rock glacier

BEGINNERS

Erosion from wind and water can change the way an area looks, but gravity can also change the way an area looks. Are you surprised that gravity can change the surface of the earth? Think about what gravity does. It pulls everything toward the center of the earth. If dirt and rocks are on a flat area, gravity pulls them, but they don't really move. But if dirt and rocks are on the side of a mountain, gravity pulls them down the side of the mountain.

Usually the soil stays in place because it sticks to the soil and rocks around it. But sometimes the pull of gravity is stronger than the forces around the soil, and the soil moves down the hill. When the soil moves slowly, so slowly that you don't even really notice it, we call that movement **creep**. But sometimes the dirt and rocks move very quickly; we call this a **landslide**.

Landslides are often triggered by earthquakes or heavy rains. If ice and snow move very quickly down the side of a mountain we call that an **avalanche**. Creep, landslides, and avalanches are all types of **mass wasting**. These are all examples of how gravity can change the way the surface of the earth looks.

- What force pulls dirt and rocks down a hill?

- What can trigger a landslide?

- What is an avalanche?

Weather related forces such as acid rain, freezing water, and wind are not the only forces wearing away the surface of the earth. Gravity is a slow but powerful force constantly pulling on everything on the surface of the earth. Gravity pulls on people and animals, which keeps us from floating away. It holds our atmosphere in place, allowing us to breathe. Yet, gravity also constantly pulls soil, rocks, trees, etc., down the sides of hills or mountains. The movement of large masses of soil is called **mass wasting**.

Some mass wasting is slow. Soil is pulled down some slopes at a rate of only an inch or so each year. This slow process is called **creep**. We cannot actually see the soil creep, but we can observe telephone poles, fence posts, and other structures that have been pushed by the moving soil so they are no longer vertical. Creep is most obvious on steep slopes with loose soil.

Mass wasting can sometimes occur very rapidly. When large amounts of rock and debris are pulled down a slope rapidly it is called a **landslide**. Landslides occur when the force of gravity overcomes the adhesion or

A landslide

FUN FACT

About 250,000 avalanches occur each year in the Alps, a mountain chain in Europe.

OBSERVING MASS WASTING

Purpose: To observe the effects of gravity on soil

Materials: baking pan, soil, rocks, water

Procedure:

1. Cover the bottom of a baking pan with soil and rocks.

2. Lift the edge of the pan one inch and observe the movement of the soil.

3. Lift it two inches and again observe the movement of the soil.

4. Continue raising the side of the pan until the soil begins to slide across the bottom. Soil moves more quickly down a steep slope due to gravity.

5. Now place the pan on a flat surface and spread the soil evenly on the bottom of the pan.

6. Again, lift the edge of the pan, but this time shake it as it is lifted to simulate an earthquake. Observe what happens.

7. Again, replace the soil and lift the edge of the pan an inch or two.

8. This time slowly pour water on the soil along the raised edge.

Questions:

- Did the soil slide at a lower angle when you shook it?

- Did more of the soil move at one time?

- How did pouring the water affect the movement of the soil?

Conclusion: This activity simulates how landslides occur during an earthquake or heavy rains. Gravity constantly pulls on the soil on hillsides, and when the ground shakes or it rains, the soil is loosened and pulled down the hill. Earthquakes and heavy rains can often cause landslides.

friction of the rock surfaces. Landslides often happen unexpectedly with little or no warning. Thus, they can be very dangerous.

Heavy rains that loosen the bonds between rock layers can trigger landslides. Earthquakes can also trigger landslides. The 1964 Alaskan earthquake triggered at least 78 landslides. And in 1959, an earthquake in Montana triggered a landslide that flowed down the mountain, across a valley, and partially up the neighboring mountainside, damming the river flowing through the valley and creating a huge lake. Mass wasting or landslides that include large amounts of ice and snow are called **avalanches**. ■

WHAT DID WE LEARN?

- What is mass wasting?
- What is slow movement of the soil and rocks down a slope called?
- What is rapid or sudden movement of the soil and rocks called?

TAKING IT FURTHER

- How does water affect mass wasting?
- How might weathermen predict when the avalanche danger is high?

Water & Erosion

ROCK GLACIERS

Mass wasting can occur slowly or quickly. One form of slow mass wasting is creep. Another form of slow mass wasting occurs in rock glaciers. As the name would imply these are formations of rock and ice. A rock glacier is different from an ice glacier in that it consists mostly of rock instead of ice and does not necessarily exist in areas with substantial snowfall.

A **rock glacier** (shown at right) can either be a core of ice that is covered with a massive amount of rock, or a massive amount of rock with ice cementing the pieces together. Sometimes a rock glacier can form when a rock slide covers a glacier and becomes imbedded in it. Other times a rock glacier forms when water flows through a pile of rock and debris and then freezes, thus holding the rocks together.

Rock glaciers are only found in areas with steep slopes and cool enough summertime temperatures so that the ice does not completely melt. Most rock glaciers in the United States are found in Colorado and Alaska. Rock glaciers are also found in other mountainous areas around the world.

Active rock glaciers contain a substantial amount of ice and move the rocks and soil slowly down the mountainsides and valleys. Rock glaciers can move from as little as a few inches per year to as much as 15 feet (5 m) per year. Inactive rock glaciers contain a small amount of ice but are no longer moving. Fossil rock glaciers have no ice remaining in them, so the rocks are generally not moving.

STREAM EROSION

The power of moving water

How does moving water cause erosion?

Words to know:

stream erosion

gradient

terracing

BEGINNERS

In lesson 28 we talked about how rain and wind can wear away the surface of a rock. This is usually a slow process. But running or flowing water can wear away rocks or soil very quickly. We call this kind of erosion **stream erosion** because water often flows in streams.

Gravity pulls water downhill just like it pulls soil, rocks, and other items downhill. The steeper the hill, the faster the water will flow. Water that is flowing in rivers and streams breaks off and picks up small bits of rocks as well as soil and other small particles. The water can carry these small pieces down a mountain all the way to a lake or even to the ocean

The faster the water is moving, the more soil and rocks it can carry. Tons of topsoil are carried away from farms each year by running water. If a farmer is trying to grow crops on a steep slope, he often cuts flat areas into the side of the hill to slow the water down. This is called **terracing**. People also grow grass and other plants on steep slopes to help hold the soil in place and prevent erosion.

- **What is stream erosion?**
- **Why does water flow downhill?**
- **Does water flow slowly or quickly down a steep hill?**

Erosion is the gradual wearing away of rocks. This can be caused by water in the form of rain, or wind blowing debris against an exposed surface. But running water is the most powerful eroding force in nature. This form of erosion is called **stream erosion**. A stream is any body of water that flows regularly, from a tiny creek to a large river. Floodwaters can be extremely destructive and erode surfaces very quickly. A canyon 100 feet (30 m) wide and 100 feet (30 m) deep through rock was eroded away in only one day by the water and mudflows triggered by the eruption of Mount St. Helens. But water does not have to be flood-strength to be a powerful force.

Water flows downhill due to the pull of gravity. The difference between the height of the source, or headwaters, and the lowest level, or mouth, is called the **gradient**. The higher the gradient the steeper the incline is and the faster water will flow down it. As water flows across the surface of the earth, it breaks off and picks up pieces of rock and other debris. The faster the water moves, the larger the pieces of debris it can carry. Eventually, as the water slows down, it can no longer carry the rocks, soil, and silt, and it drops the particles, usually at the bottom of a lake or ocean.

Slow moving streams that flow along relatively level ground tend to move in long curves that resemble a snake, like the one pictured here. But even slow moving streams erode and deposit dirt, sand, and other particles. The soil is eroded from the outside of the bank's curves where the water is flowing more quickly and deposited on the insides of the curves where the water flows more slowly. This action constantly changes the course of the river.

Often, when rivers and streams flood and overflow their banks, they deposit rich silt along the edges of the stream as the waters recede. This flooding cycle has been very beneficial to farmers along the Nile, Ganges, and Yangtze Rivers for hundreds of years. However, flooding can carry huge amounts of eroded soil away and can also cause extensive damage.

According to the U.S. Department of Agriculture, the United States loses more than 2 billion tons of topsoil each year to erosion. Topsoil is not easily replaced, so farmers and other conservationists work to keep soil from eroding away. One way that farmers conserve soil is to plow cross-ways to the flow of the water to help slow down the flow. In very steep areas, terracing is used to control the flow of the water.

Terracing is the cutting of level areas into the side of the hill so that the fields resemble giant stairs (shown at left). Also, farmers often alternate crops so that one section of a field is planted with tall plants such as corn and the next section is planted with short ground cover crops such as alfalfa. This also helps to stop the erosion of the topsoil by slowing the flow of the water. Finally, steep hillsides are often planted with grass or other ground cover that has spreading roots to help hold the soil in place. ■

WHAT DID WE LEARN?

- What is the most powerful eroding force?
- How does gravity cause stream erosion?
- What is the gradient of a river?

TAKING IT FURTHER

- Why are farmers concerned about soil erosion?
- What are some steps farmers take to prevent water from eroding their topsoil?
- Besides water, what other natural force can erode topsoil?
- What can farmers do to protect their topsoil from wind erosion?
- Why do lakes and reservoirs have to be dredged, emptied, and dug out periodically?

TERRACING

Purpose: To demonstrate how terracing prevents erosion

Materials: three baking dishes, soil, plant material, cup of water, books

Procedure:

1. Fill three baking dishes with soil.

2. In the first, press the soil firmly against the bottom of the dish.

3. In the second dish, mix leaves, grass, or other plant material into the soil and press it against the bottom of the dish. Also, sprinkle some of the plant material across the surface of the soil.

4. In the third dish, build terraces in the soil, pressing each level firmly against the bottom of the dish.

5. Elevate one end of each dish several inches by setting the end on a thick book.

The three dishes should be elevated the same amount.

6. Slowly pour water along the top edge of the soil in each dish. Compare the amount of soil erosion seen in each dish.

Questions:

- Which dish experienced the most erosion?

Trays 1 & 2

Tray 3

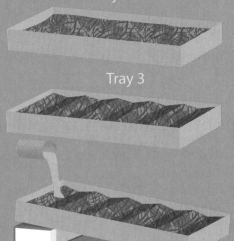

- Which experienced the least erosion?
- What effect did the leaves and grass have on the flow of the water?
- How did this affect the erosion of the soil?
- How did the terracing affect the flow of the water?
- How did terracing affect the erosion of the soil?
- What do you think is the best way to prevent soil erosion due to running water?

Conclusion: Soil erosion should be most obvious in the pan without plants or terraces. It should be least obvious in the pan with the terraces. Terraces help to slow down the water so it cannot carry the soil away as quickly.

Water & Erosion

STREAM EROSION

Purpose: To observe the effects of stream erosion

Materials: soil, water, oven, 3 paper cups, pencil

Procedure:

1. Get a half cup of soil from your yard and add enough water to make a thick mud.

2. Form the mud into 8 equal sized balls and bake your mud balls in an oven at 275°F for 1 hour or until they are dry.

3. Prepare 3 paper cups. Use a pencil to punch 8 holes evenly spaced around the side of cup A near the bottom so that water will drain out the sides of the cup.

4. Use the pencil to poke 10 or 12 small holes into the bottom of cup B .

5. Punch 4 larger holes in the bottom of cup C .

6. Place four of the dirt balls into cup A and place cup A in a baking dish.

7. Hold cup B about 4 inches above cup A.

8. Pour 1 cup of water through cup B and let the water rain down on the balls in cup A. After the water has drained out of cup A, examine the balls. How do they look compared to how they looked before running the water over them? Are pieces broken off? Have any of them crumbled? Examine the water in the baking dish. Are there any small pieces of rocks and soil in the dish?

9. Clean out the baking dish and cup A so you can use them for the second part of the experiment.

10. Place the last four dirt balls into cup A and place this cup in the baking dish.

11. Hold cup C, the one with the bigger holes, about 4 inches above cup A.

12. Pour 2 cups of water through cup C into cup A. After the water has drained out of cup A, examine the balls. How do these balls compare to the balls from the first experiment? Are they more eroded? How did the flow of water in the second experiment compare to the flow of water in the first experiment?

Conclusion: The water should have been flowing faster in the second experiment. Also, there was more water. So you should have seen more erosion of the second set of dirt balls. Imagine what would have happened to the dirt balls if they had been bombarded with water from the sink in a constant flow. The balls would have been completely disintegrated. Thus, you can see that flowing water greatly affects erosion.

FUN FACT

In the 1930s the Western United States experienced one of the worst droughts in recorded history. The farmers' fields dried out and the wind began to blow. This period of time is often called the Great Dust Bowl. Sometimes the wind picked up so much dirt that giant clouds of dust engulfed entire towns. Farming practices changed significantly as a result of the Dust Bowl. Today's farms are much less likely to experience a dust bowl as severe as in the 1930s.

Water & Erosion

Soil

Isn't it just dirt?

LESSON

31

What is soil made of?

Words to know:

humus

Challenge words:

porosity

permeability

Beginners

In the last lesson you learned that soil is very important to farmers and that they don't want rushing water to wash it away. Erosion of rocks by wind and water can be very damaging, but erosion is also important. The tiny bits of rock that are worn away by erosion help to make new soil.

Soil is made up of bits of sand, clay, silt, and dead plants and animals. The sand and clay are bits that have been broken off of rocks by erosion. Silt comes from riverbeds and the bits of plants and animals get into the soil when plants wither and animals die and then decay.

Soil is needed for growing crops. It provides nutrients (food) for the plants and gives the plants a place for their roots to grow. If the same kinds of plants are grown in the same soil year after year, the nutrients can get used up, so farmers add nutrients by adding animal waste or fertilizer to the soil. This helps make the soil better so plants will grow well.

- What is soil made of?

- Where do bits of sand and clay come from?

- Is erosion always bad?

S oil is fun for making mud pies, is home for earthworms, and makes it necessary to wash your car. But soil is also a precious resource needed for growing plants. Erosion plays two major parts with respect to soil. Erosion can devastate an area by moving topsoil away and depositing it in the ocean where it can no longer be used to support plant life. On the other hand, God designed erosion to play a crucial role in the formation of new soil as well.

Soil is formed from sand, silt, clay, and bits of decayed plants and animals. Weathering, particularly wind and water, breaks apart bits of rock to form the sand and clay that is used in the making of new soil. The ratio of sand to silt and clay depends greatly on the rocks in the area. Areas with mostly quartz rocks will have sandy soil. Areas with large deposits of mica and feldspar tend to have higher amounts of clay in the soil. Areas near rivers tend to have silt that is deposited during flood stages. Regardless of the type of soil, whether sandy or clay, it must contain **humus**—decayed plant material—in order to grow plants.

In areas that are not cultivated, plants wither, decay, and return nutrients to the soil. Farmland, however, must have nutrients added back into the soil since cultivating generally removes most of the plant material from the soil. Farmers add nutrients back into the soil by applying chemical fertilizers or by spreading animal compost (waste) on the soil. Sometimes, farmers grow crops just to plow them into the soil and thus replace lost nutrients. Other times, farmers grow crops such as beans, peanuts, or sweet potatoes that enrich the soil as they grow.

God originally created the earth with topsoil. The Garden of Eden would not

EXAMINING SOIL

Purpose: To examine what soil is made of

Materials: potting soil, yard soil, magnifying glass

Procedure:

1. Spread out a small amount of potting soil on a flat surface and closely examine it with a magnifying glass. What do you observe?

2. Now examine a small amount of soil from your yard with the magnifying glass. What observations do you make? Was it a lighter color?

Questions:

*   How did the potting soil differ from the soil in your yard?

*   Which soil do you think will be better for growing plants?

Conclusion: You probably noticed a black color, moist texture, lots of plant material, white specks (vermiculite for holding in moisture), and maybe some small rocks in the potting soil. The yard soil probably had more "dirt" or ground up rock, less plant material, more rocks, and a drier texture.

The best way to improve soil, to make it better for growing plants, is to add more humus or decayed plant material to the soil. Plant material is clearly visible in this sample of potting soil above.

have been able to support the wonderful plants described in Genesis 1–2 without good soil. Much of the soil was moved around during the Genesis Flood, and other soil has been washed into lakes, rivers, and oceans by stream erosion. However, since that time, some soil has been created by weathering. The weathering of rocks and the decomposing of plants and animals are wonderful ways God designed the earth to replace lost soil.

Weathering that produces new soil is a slow process. However, other soil has been created more quickly. Volcanic eruptions often deposit large quantities of nutrient-rich ash, which is able to support plant life within only a few years after the eruption. Also, retreating glaciers often leave large amounts of fertile soil behind.

Despite the negative effects of erosion, God has created ways for life to flourish on the earth. ■

FUN FACT

An average soil sample contains 45% minerals, 25% water, 25% air, and 5% organic matter.

WHAT DID WE LEARN?

- What are the major components of soil?
- What is the most important element in soil for encouraging plant growth?

TAKING IT FURTHER

- What type of rocks would you expect to find near an area with sandy soil?
- What type of rocks would you expect to find near an area with clay soil?
- How does a river that regularly floods, such as the Nile, restore lost topsoil?
- What are some ways that farmers restore nutrients to the soil?

Water & Erosion

SOIL STUDY

Soil plays a very important role in life on earth. Without productive topsoil, plants would not grow and life would cease to exist. You have already learned that the composition of soil varies from one area to another depending on the rocks that are abundant in the area. The acid level of the soil also varies from one area to another. In areas that receive large amounts of rainfall, the water tends to react with chemicals in the soil to produce acid. So soil in wet areas is generally more acidic than soil in dry areas. Also, large amounts of rainfall can wash away some of the nutrients in the soil. So soil in dry areas may actually be more fertile than soil in wetter areas.

Another factor that can affect plant growth is porosity. **Porosity** is a measure of the pores or air spaces in the soil. If there are very large air spaces, the soil is said to have high porosity or to be very porous. Porosity affects how quickly water flows through the soil. The rate at which water flows through soil is called **permeability**. The water will flow through porous soil very quickly so it has high permeability. If there are only very small air spaces the soil is nonporous or has low permeability. Water will sit on top of this kind of soil and will drain very slowly. Plants generally do better in soil with medium permeability so that water drains through the soil but not too quickly.

Purpose: To determine what kind of soil you have in your yard

Materials: soil from your yard, four paper cups, newspaper, colander, fine-mesh strainer, pencil, baking sheet, stopwatch, measuring cup, "Permeability of Soil" worksheet

Procedure:

1. Get 2–3 cups of soil from your yard or garden.

2. Number four paper cups from 1 to 4.

3. Place about ½ cup of soil in cup 1.

4. Place a sheet of newspaper on the counter, and then place a colander on top of the newspaper.

5. Pour the rest of your soil into the colander. Shake the colander until no more soil will fall out. Pour what is left in the colander into cup 2.

6. Pour the soil from the newspaper into a fine mesh strainer.

7. Hold the strainer over a second piece of newspaper and shake it until no more soil will fall out.

8. Pour what is in the strainer into cup 3 and pour what is on the newspaper into cup 4. You have now separated your soil according the sizes of the particles in the soil.

9. We are now going to test the permeability of each of your soil samples. Make sure you

have the same amount of soil in each cup by removing soil from the cups that have more soil until all four cups have the same amount.

10. Follow the directions below and record your observations on the "Permeability of Soil" worksheet.

11. Use a sharp pencil to make four holes in the bottom of each cup. Try to make all the holes as close to the same size as possible.

12. Set two pencils parallel to each other in a baking sheet. Set cup 1 on top of the pencils.

13. You are going to pour 1 cup (8 ounces) of water through your soil sample. Use a stopwatch to time how long it takes for water to flow through your soil sample. Start the timer as soon as water starts dripping out the

bottom and stop it when water quits dripping. Record this time on the worksheet under "Water Flow Time."

14. Pour the water from the baking sheet into the measuring cup to see how many ounces of water flowed through your sample. Some of the water will remain in the soil. Record this amount on your worksheet under "Water Flow Amount."

15. Repeat this procedure with each of the other samples, recording your time and volume of water for each trial on the worksheet.

16. Finally, calculate the permeability of each sample by dividing the volume of water by the flow time to give you ounces per second. Answer the questions at the bottom of the worksheet.

GRAND CANYON

Lots of time, little water or lots of water, little time?

LESSON

32

How was Grand Canyon formed?

BEGINNERS

One of the most beautiful places on earth is Grand Canyon in Arizona. It is a very deep canyon with steep walls that reveal many layers of rock. When you look at Grand Canyon you can see that moving water has worn away a huge amount of rock.

Some scientists believe that the river that flows through the bottom of the canyon wore away the rock little by little over millions of years. They believe that a little bit of water and a lot of time made the canyon. But the Bible gives us the true history of the earth. The Bible tells us that the whole earth was covered with a giant flood. It is more likely that the canyon was carved out by rushing floodwaters in a relatively short time. Creation scientists believe that the canyon was made by a lot of water in a little bit of time, from a huge dam that broke shortly after the floodwaters receded.

Scientists have found many fossils of sea creatures in the layers of rock in the canyon. So we know that the area was covered with a sea sometime in the past. This agrees with the Bible's account of the Flood during Noah's time.

- What are the two main ideas for how Grand Canyon was formed?

- Which idea agrees with the Bible?

- Where could a lot of water have come from to make the canyon?

One of the most fascinating areas to study on earth is Grand Canyon in Arizona. This wonder of nature is 277 miles (446 km) long, 4 to 18 miles (6.5–29 km) wide and up to 1 mile (1.6 km) deep. This huge canyon is a wonder to behold and is also the source of great debate between evolutionists and creationists.

Evolutionists claim that the Colorado River, which flows through the bottom of the canyon, eroded the rocks around it to form the canyon over millions of years. Evolutionists also claim that the many layers of sedimentary rock observed in the canyon walls were deposited slowly over hundreds of millions of years prior to this slow erosion. They claim that the evidence in Grand Canyon is very clear that the earth is very old and that the canyon was formed by "a little water and a lot of time."

On the other hand, scientists who accept the biblical account claim just the opposite. They say that the evidence points to "lots of water and a little time." The many layers deposited in the canyon walls contain numerous fossils. These most likely were deposited by the great Flood of Noah's day. Most of the fossils are sea creatures—indicating an ocean once covered the entire area. Genesis 7:19–20 says, "And the waters prevailed exceedingly on the earth, and all the high hills under the whole heaven were covered. The waters prevailed fifteen cubits upward, and the mountains were covered." So even the driest parts of Arizona were covered with water during the Flood.

In many places in Grand Canyon, the rock layers are bent, or as a geologist would say, "folded," This folding has taken place without cracking the rock. Folds like this indicate that the folding had to happen soon after the layers were deposited, while the material was still soft and pliable. This shows that the deposition and the upheaval responsible for the folding were in fact one event. If the folding took place millions of years after the material was deposited, the soil would have hardened and would have broken and cracked when it was uplifted.

Creation scientists believe that a very large lake formed above the current location of the canyon after the Flood. Sometime later, the land dam holding back the lake broke, resulting in a huge flow of water. This would have resulted in the erosion that carved the huge canyon. Both evolutionists and creationists agree that erosion

GRAND CANYON MODEL

Look at the picture of Grand Canyon on the previous page. Notice the beauty of this area. The canyon is not just a crevice with steep walls; there are many gorges and cutouts that run perpendicular to the flow of the river. Make a model of Grand Canyon using modeling clay. Build the model on a piece of paper and color the river at the bottom of the canyon with a marker.

Moving water is one of the most destructive forces in nature, especially if it is moving quickly. Fast moving water can cut through rock very rapidly. However, slow moving water erodes rock very slowly. So, do you think Grand Canyon was formed quickly by lots of fast moving water, or slowly by a slow moving river?

Water & Erosion

Folded rock layers

formed the canyon, yet they disagree on the amount of water and the time needed to accomplish this.

Evolutionists have a difficult time supporting some of their ideas. For example, where did all of the eroded material from the canyon go? If a relatively small, slow moving river eroded millions of cubic yards of rock, it should have deposited the silt and debris somewhere within or just outside the canyon, yet no such deposits have been found. On the other hand, a large flood of water would have carried the debris far away.

Also, radiometric dating techniques used by evolutionists show lower rock layers to be 700–800 million years old. These same dating techniques have shown the upper, supposedly more recent lava flows, to be 2 billion years old. These dating techniques are obviously flawed and unreliable. They do not prove the canyon to be millions or billions of years old.

Many of the fossils found in Grand Canyon indicate a fast moving water current was present when the plants and animals were covered. This does not fit with the uniformitarian theory that says all the fossil layers were formed slowly over millions of years.

Although scientists see the same evidence, they draw very different conclusions about Grand Canyon. But God's Word tells us we can trust His wisdom rather than man's. (For more information on Grand Canyon and how it confirms the biblical record, see www.answersingenesis.org/go/grand-canyon.) ■

WHAT DID WE LEARN?

- What is the main controversy between evolutionists and creationists concerning the formation of Grand Canyon?

- What evidence shows radiometric dating methods to be unreliable?

TAKING IT FURTHER

- What event at the eruption of Mount St. Helens supports the biblical view of how Grand Canyon was formed?

- How can scientists look at similar data and draw different conclusions?

- How can we know what to believe when scientists disagree?

EVIDENCE OF CATASTROPHE

Water & Erosion

Creation scientists have been studying the aftermath of the Mount St. Helens eruption for more than 20 years now and have concluded that the evidence provided there confirms that a time of great catastrophe could account for much of the geologic features we see. Specifically, the evidence from Mount St. Helens supports the ideas that vast amounts of sedimentary rock could have been formed in a short time period and the floodwaters could account for many of the canyons we see today. These conclusions support many of the biblically-based ideas about Grand Canyon. However, Mount St. Helens is not the only source for these ideas. Grand Canyon itself indicates a massive flood took place there in the past and supports what the Bible says as well.

Grand Canyon stands as a monument to the biblical record if you only have the eyes to see it. Grand Canyon is special. Since so much of the rock has been stripped away, we can see the rock layers from the very bottom to the top and see a history of creation, Noah's Flood, and the time since the receding of the floodwaters.

As you learned in lesson 13, evolutionists have developed what they call the geologic column to describe the long time periods represented in the fossil layers. In Grand Canyon many of these layers of rock are easily visible, yet they do not tell of millions of years; instead they tell of a great catastrophe. There are many areas where layers of rock are found piled on top of perfectly flat lower layers. If the lower layer had been eroded for millions of years, it would not be perfectly flat. However, floodwaters could have quickly eroded the lower layers and then deposited the next layers of sediment. These layers of rock are not isolated to a small area either. These flat layers extend for up to 200 miles, showing that the water that deposited them covered a large area.

The fossils found in Grand Canyon also speak of catastrophe and flood. Fossilized footprints found in the Coconino Sandstone indicate that the animals who made the prints were still alive and walking across wet sand, and then their prints were quickly covered over with sediment. This is not something that happens slowly over millions of years. Also, in an area called Nautiloid Canyon there is a large area containing fossils of hundreds of nautiloids—sea creatures with cigar-shaped shells. All of the fossils show the shells oriented from north to south. This indicates a fast-moving current when these animals were buried. This is consistent with a flood and not with slow deposition over long periods of time.

As we study the special features on earth such as volcanoes, canyons, and fossils, we see more and more evidence that God's Word is true.

Fossilized reptile footprints found in sandstone layers in Grand Canyon

One of the hundreds of nautiloids found in Nautiloid Canyon

CAVES

Underground wonderlands

LESSON

33

How are caves formed?

Words to know:

lava tube

sea cave

sandstone cave

solution cave

stalactite

stalagmite

column

flowstone

curtain

BEGINNERS

We have learned that flowing water can carry soil away and that it can erode rocks to make more soil. Flowing water plays an important role in the formations inside of caves, too. When water flows through a special kind of rock called *limestone*, it dissolves some chemicals from the rocks. This water may eventually end up in a cavern underground. As water evaporates inside the cave, it leaves the chemicals behind. These chemicals build up and make beautiful formations inside the cave.

Sometimes the chemical builds up on the ceiling of the cave making rocks that look like icicles. These formations are called **stalactites**. Other times the chemical builds up on the floor of the cave making formations called **stalagmites**. And sometimes the stalactites and stalagmites grow together to form a **column**.

If water flows over the surface of the cave instead of dripping from the ceiling, it can leave the chemicals spread over the walls or floor of the cave. This formation is called **flowstone**. The chemical in limestone is white, and many of the formations found in caves are white. But impurities can get mixed into the water and the formations in caves are often brown, orange, yellow, or even red. What a beautiful sight!

- What is the name given to the rocks that form when chemicals build up on the ceiling of a cave?

- What is the name given to rocks that form when chemicals build up on the floor of a cave?

- How are these special rocks formed?

aves are caverns underground. They can be small or large, but they are almost always filled with beautiful formations. There are about 17,000 caves in the United States. Over 200 of these are "show caves" that are open for public tours.

Caves are divided into four categories. Lava tubes are caverns that were formed as the outer layers of lava cooled while the hot lava continued to flow through it. After the volcano stopped erupting, the lava flowed away, leaving a hollow tube surrounded by cooled rock. Moving water has formed two other kinds of caves. Sea caves were formed by the pounding of the waves against the rocks along the shore. And sandstone caves were formed at the base of cliffs by moving water.

The fourth and most common kind of cave is a solution cave. These are caves made primarily from limestone, dolomite, marble, and gypsum. The causes of solution cave formation are another geological event about which scientists disagree. It is obvious that many existing caves are being enlarged by erosion due to underground water flow. However, there are several ideas about how these caves originally formed.

Some creation scientists link cave formation to the Flood. Large amounts of acidic water could have seeped through limestone deposits, rapidly forming caverns underground. Evolutionists believe that the slow process of dissolving limestone by carbonic acid over millions of years is what formed most of these caves. We see both ground water erosion and carbonic acid dissolution occurring in caves today.

Regardless of how the caverns themselves were formed, we can easily observe how the many beautiful structures (called *speleothems*) inside caves are formed. Water, passing through limestone, dissolves some of the minerals in the stones. As the water drips into the cave, the water evaporates, leaving calcium carbonate (calcite) behind. This mineral is the main ingredient in limestone.

Calcite deposits in caves can take many forms. When the formation hangs down from the ceiling, it is called a stalactite. When it builds up from the floor of the

Water & Erosion

FUN FACT

How do you remember which formation is which? You can remember that stalacTITES hold "tightly" to the ceiling and stalagMITES are something you "might" trip over. Another way to remember these: *stala**g**mite* has a *g*, and is attached to the ground; *stala**c**tite* has a *c*, and is attached to the ceiling.

cavern, it is called a stalagmite. When a stalactite and a stalagmite grow together into one formation, it is called a column.

Other times, a thin layer of water flows over the surface of the cave leaving behind wavy formations like in the picture here. These formations are called flowstones. Flowstones that hang from the ceiling are called curtains. Flowstones can also be formed on the walls and floors of caves.

Pure calcite is white and many formations in caves are white. But impurities often get mixed into the calcite, giving these formations many beautiful

GROWING STALAGMITES & STALACTITES

Purpose: To grow your own stalagmites and stalactites

Materials: hot water, Epsom salt, string

Procedure:

1. Fill two cups ¾ full with hot water.

2. Stir Epsom salt into each cup until no more will dissolve.

3. Cut a 16-inch piece of string and completely submerge the string in one of the cups, then remove it.

4. Place one end of the string in each cup.

5. Place the cups on a piece of cardboard so that the string hangs down a little between the cups without touching the

cardboard. Place this set-up in an area where it will not be disturbed for several days.

6. Observe the string and the cardboard every day for several days. After several days, what do you observe?

Conclusion: Crystals should be forming on the string and on the cardboard below it. This is a similar

process to the one in which stalactites and stalagmites are formed. In a cave, water dissolves minerals in the limestone. As the water reaches the ceiling of the cave, some of it drips to the floor. As the water evaporates from the floor or ceiling, it leaves calcite crystals behind. These crystals build up on top of each other and form stalactites and stalagmites.

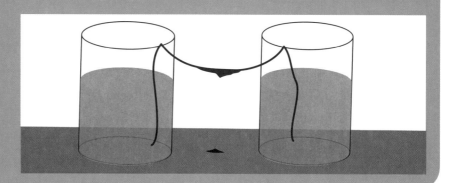

colors including brown, orange, yellow, and red.

Evolutionists claim that cave formations grow very slowly, about one cubic inch (16.4 cc) in 150 years. And in dry caves, the calcite formation is very slow. However, many wet caves have very active calcite formation. Crystal Spring Dome, located in Carlsbad Caverns, experiences calcite growth of about 2.5 cubic inches (41 cc) per year. Also, bats have been found encased in stalagmites and stalactites. A bat that became trapped in a stalactite or a stalagmite would have decayed before being encased if formation were very slow. However, bats that are completely covered with calcite had to have been caught where the formation of calcite was very rapid.

Although evolutionists point to the many formations in caves as evidence of an old earth, we can observe that rapid formation is very possible. Conditions after the Flood would have been much wetter than today, resulting in rapid calcite formation in many caves. Caves demonstrate the truth of God's Word; they do not refute it. (For more information on cave formation, see www.answersingenesis.org/go/caves.) ■

WHAT DID WE LEARN?

- How are the beautiful formations in caves formed?
- What is a stalactite?
- What is a stalagmite?

TAKING IT FURTHER

- What evidence do we have that formations in caves can develop rapidly?
- Why is it likely that calcite formations would have formed rapidly after the Flood?
- Besides in caves, where can calcite deposits be found?

CAVE RESEARCH

Do a research project on your favorite cave. Find out all you can about it and make a presentation to share what you have learned with your friends and family. If you do not have a favorite cave, you can choose one from the list below.

- Kazumura Cave—Hawaii
- Mammoth Cave—Kentucky
- Anemone Cave—Maine
- Carlsbad Caverns—New Mexico
- Lava Beds National Monument—California
- Waitomo Cave—New Zealand
- Dead Sea Caves—Israel

ROCKS & MINERALS COLLECTION: FINAL PROJECT

Putting it all together

Do you want to become a rock hound?

You have learned about the wonderful planet we call earth. This amazing globe was designed by God to be the perfect place for all living creatures. In the beginning, God created it "very good," but Adam's sin brought a curse on the land, and the Genesis Flood reshaped the surface of the planet. Our beautiful home has mountains and ocean basins, rocks, streams, and hills. The beauty of caves, volcanoes, and geysers all help us recognize God's majesty and glory, and remind us of His judgment on sin. To help you remember the wonders of the planet around you, take what you have learned about rocks, gems, and minerals and make a display to share with others.

To become a rock hound, all you have to do is collect rocks you find on the ground and learn more about them. If you want, and you have permission, you can dig for rocks with some simple tools including a hand shovel and a mason's hammer. Be sure to wear eye protection! You will also want to have a box in which to store your samples and a rocks and minerals guidebook to help you identify the different rocks you collect. Being a rock hound can be a very enjoyable hobby. ∎

ROCKS & MINERALS COLLECTION

Step 1:

Collect samples of rocks and minerals. Be sure to get at least one or more samples from each of the following categories.

Minerals: Minerals are naturally occurring solids that are inorganic and have a definite atomic structure.

- Native Minerals—Pure element having only one kind of atom Examples include gold, silver, copper, tin, and iron. If samples are too expensive to put into your display, find a picture to include.

- Compound—Two or more elements bonded together. Examples include salt, alum, and quartz.

Gems: These are minerals that are valued for their perfect cleavage and brilliance.

- Natural gems have formed inside the earth with no help from man.

- Artificial gems have been developed by man as an inexpensive substitute for the natural gems. They often contain the same materials and crystal structure.

- Gems may be too valuable to include in your display, so find pictures of gems and include the pictures in your collection.

Rocks: These contain one or more minerals and/or organic materials.

- Igneous—formed by the cooling of liquid magma or melted rock

- Sedimentary—formed from bits of broken rock, shells and other material

- Metamorphic—formed by transformation of igneous or sedimentary rock by heat and pressure over time

Places to look for samples include:

1. Your kitchen
2. Around your house
3. In your yard
4. On a hike
5. Jewelry
6. Coins

Step 2:

Once you have collected several samples, identify each sample using a rocks and minerals guidebook, if necessary. You may want to perform some of the tests you learned about in lesson 16 to help you identify your samples.

Step 3:

Prepare your display. You can display your samples in many different ways. You can glue the samples or photos to poster board or tag board; you can use a box and make dividers from cardboard to separate sections of the box; or you can purchase a plastic container with dividers or small compartments. Maybe you have a better idea for displaying your samples. The important thing is to make it neat and easy to show to someone else.

Group your samples together by type. For example, make one part of your display for minerals, another for gems, another for igneous rocks, etc. Neatly label each sample with what it is and where you found it.

Optional:

Include some of the following:

- Possible uses for each sample

- Estimated value if the sample is valuable

- Chemical makeup of compounds

- Any other interesting facts about the sample

Step 4:

Show your collection to someone else and share the wonder of God's creation with them.

Water & Erosion

WHAT DID WE LEARN?

- What are the three types of rocks?
- What is a native mineral?

TAKING IT FURTHER

- What are some of the greatest or most interesting things you learned from your study of our planet earth?
- Read Genesis chapters 1 and 2. Discuss what was created on each day and how each part completes the whole.
- What earth science topic would you like to learn more about? (Visit your library or search the Answers in Genesis web site.)

Water & Erosion

CONCLUSION

The wonder of our planet earth

Recognizing God's hand in designing our planet

Water & Erosion

The planet earth was specially designed by God to support life. No other known planet can support life. Although we cannot prove scientifically that God created the earth because we cannot recreate that event, the Bible tells us that He created it, and we can see that the evidence points to a Designer. The complexity of the earth and of all life on it demands that an Intelligent Designer, not natural processes, made the world around us. We can be very thankful that we can know and love that Designer—Jesus, the Creator of the universe.

What have you learned in your study of the earth that has demonstrated the truth of the Bible and revealed God's design to you? Make a list of these items.

Read Psalm 139:8–10. Then pray and thank God for these revelations.

Where can you look to see more evidence of God's mighty hand on the earth? Keep your eyes open for more examples of God's design for heaven and earth. ■

GLOSSARY

Active volcano   One that has erupted at least once in the past 50 years

Actual height   Difference between the elevations of the summit and the base

Aftershock   Smaller earthquakes occurring after a major earthquake

Astronomy   Study of space

Avalanche   Sudden movement of large amounts of ice and snow

Caldera   Crater or bowl-shaped depression at the mouth of a volcano

Calving   Pieces of ice breaking off a glacier into the water

Carbon-14 dating   Dating of organic materials by measuring carbon-14 levels

Cast fossil   Fossilized imprint of a plant or animal

Chemical rock   Sedimentary rock formed by chemicals precipitating from water

Cinder cone volcano   Formed from mostly ash and cinders

Cleavage   When a rock breaks in a straight line

Column   Formation when a stalactite and stalagmite grow together

Composite volcano   Formed from alternating layers of lava and ash

Continental glacier   Giant ice sheet

Core   Center of the earth

Creep   Slow movement of dirt and rocks

Crust   Outer shell of the earth

Curtains   Flowstone that hangs from the ceiling of a cave

Depositional mountains   Mountains formed from debris

Dormant volcano   One that has not erupted in the past 50 years, but could erupt again

Earthquake   Rapid movement of the earth's crust

Elevation   Height of summit above sea level

Environmental geology   Study of the effects of humans on the earth's environment

Epicenter   Location on surface of the earth above the focus

Erosional mountains   Mountains that have been formed by erosion

Extinct volcano   One that is not expected to erupt again

Extrusive   Igneous rocks that form on top of the earth's crust

Fault   Crack in the earth's crust

First law of thermodynamics   Matter cannot be created or destroyed, only changed in form

Flowstone   Thin layer of minerals covering a surface of a cave

Focus   Location of the origin of an earthquake

Fold and fault mountains   Mountains formed by movement of tectonic plates

Foliated rocks   Metamorphic rocks that break in straight lines along crystal structures

Fossil fuel   Fuel formed from dead plants or animals

Fossil   Rock or mineral structure that has the same shape as a formerly living plant or animal

Fracture   When a rock breaks in a smooth curve

Fragmental rock   Sedimentary rock formed when fragments are glued together

Frost heaving   Process of freezing and thawing that pushes rocks up to the surface

Fumarole   Steam vent where steam escapes from underground

Gem   Minerals that can be polished and reflect light

Geology   Study of the earth

Geophysics   Study of the earth's magnetic fields, heat flow, gravity, seismic waves

Geothermal   Heat from inside the earth

Geyser   Erupting steam and water due to underground pressure of super-heated water

Glacial erratic   Very large boulders moved by a glacier

Gradient   Difference in height between the headwaters and mouth of a river or stream

Hot spring/Hot pool   Heated water that flows up from underground

Humus   Decayed plant matter

Hydrology   Study of water

Igneous   Rocks formed from magma

Index fossils   Particular fossils used to date sedimentary rocks

Intrusive   Igneous rocks that form inside the earth's crust

Landslide   Sudden movement of large amounts of dirt and rocks

Lateral moraine   Debris pushed up along the sides of a glacier

Lava tube   Cavern formed by volcanic eruption

Lava   Liquid rock on top of the earth's surface

Lithosphere   The solid earth

Luster   Quality and intensity of reflected light

Magma   Liquid rock inside the earth's crust

Mantle   Liquid and semirigid part of the earth between the crust and the core

Mass wasting   Movement of rocks and soil due to gravity

Metamorphic   Rocks formed when atomic structures of igneous or sedimentary rocks are changed

Meteorology   Study of the atmosphere

Mineral   Naturally occurring inorganic material with crystalline structure

Mineralogy   Study of minerals in the earth's crust, moon rocks, crystals

Mold fossil   Fossil made when animal or plant material is replaced with rock

Mud pot   Hot pool containing more dirt than water

Native mineral/Native element   Minerals containing only one element

Paleontology   Study of fossils and ancient life forms

Physical geology   Study of rocks, magma, the earth's core, land formations

Piedmont glacier   Glacier formed when two valley glaciers meet

Plate tectonics   Theory that the earth's crust is composed of several floating plates

Polystrate fossil   Fossil passing vertically through many layers of sedimentary rock

Radiometric dating   Dating of igneous and metamorphic rocks by measuring radioactive elements

Rodinia   Original landmass

Sandstone cave   Cave formed at the base of cliffs by moving water

Sea cave   Cavern formed by erosion due to waves

Second law of thermodynamics   All objects tend to go to a state of rest or disorganization

Sedimentary   Rocks formed from sediment

Sedimentology   Study of sediment deposits/fossils

Seismograph   Equipment used for detecting earthquakes

Shield volcano   Formed from mostly lava

Solution cave   Cavern formed by erosion due to underground water

Spouter   Active hot pool that shoots out small amounts of water

Stalactite   Calcite formation on ceiling of a cave

Stalagmite   Calcite formation on the floor of a cave

Strata   Layers of sediment that form sedimentary rock

Stream erosion   Weathering or erosion due to running water

Striations   Scratches made in the ground by a moving glacier

Terminal moraine   Debris pushed ahead of a glacier

Terracing   Cutting of level areas into a slope

Tsunami   Giant waves triggered by earthquake

Uniformitarianism   Belief that all changes have been brought about by the processes we see today

Valley glacier   Glacier that flows into a valley

Weathering/Erosion   Natural breaking apart of rocks by chemical or mechanical means

Zone of accumulation   Part of glacier where snow does not melt

Zone of wastage   Part of glacier where the snow melts

CHALLENGE GLOSSARY

Andesitic volcano   Volcano formed where subduction is occurring

Anticline   Upward formation due to sideways pressure

Basaltic volcano   Volcano formed when tectonic plates move apart

Basin   Depression formed by downward pressure

Breccia   Sedimentary rock formed with jagged clasts

Clasts   Fragments of rock cemented together to form sedimentary rock

Conglomerate   Sedimentary rock formed with smooth clasts

Coprolite   Fossilized animal dung

Dome   Formation due to upward pressure

Evolution   Worldview allowing only naturalistic causes for everything we see

Foot wall   Rock below a fault

Gastrolith   Smooth stones found inside fossilized animals

Geologic column   Twelve groups of fossils the evolutionists claim represent the geologic time line

Hanging wall   Rock above a fault

Lithification   Process which turns sediment into sedimentary rock

Matrix   The material cementing sedimentary rock particles together

Monocline   Formation due to upward pressure on one side and downward pressure on the other

Normal fault   Hanging wall moves down with respect to footwall

Oxidation   Chemical reaction involving bonding with oxygen

Permeability   The rate at which water flows through soil

Porosity   Measure of the pores or air spaces in soil

Porphyritic   Rock containing both large and small crystals

Rifting   Where two tectonic plates move away from each other

Rock glacier   Formation containing mostly rocks held together by ice

Strike-slip fault   Where two plates move horizontally against each other

Subduction/Subduction zone   Area where one tectonic plate slides over another

Syncline   Downward formation due to sideways pressure

Theistic evolution   Worldview that God used the process of evolution to bring about what we see today

Thrust fault/Reverse fault   Hanging wall moves up with respect to footwall

Vesicles   Holes or air spaces found in igneous rock

Index